Master Notion: break the cycle by creating your own productivity

Master Notion:
break the cycle by creating your own productivity tools

A concise guide to learn Notion fast and build useful tools.

Bronek Carr

Table of Contents

Preface 9
About this book 9
Requirements 10
Contact Information 10
Disclaimer 10
Part 1: 11
Context and basics 11
Chapter 1: Introduction to Notion and how to set it up. 12
Working through this book 12
What is Notion 13
Installing Notion 14
Get clear and ready 14
Chapter Summary 16
Chapter 2 – Working with blocks by building a Reference Area and Today focused Task Management Page 17
What are Notion blocks? 18
   Text Blocks 18
Building a Reference Page (Create a Notion page) 19
Building a "Today" Dashboard (Create a Notion page, with links to others) 24
Chapter Summary 29
Part 2: 30
Chapter 3 – Creating a database, with templates and different views for a personal recipe repertoire. 31
How to create: 32
Small, important tangent on Databases within Notion 32
   Table View (/table view) 33

    Board View (/board view)..33

    Gallery View (/gallery view)..33

    List View (/list view)...33

    Calendar View (/calendar view)...33

    Timeline View (/timeline view)..33

    Linked view of a database (/linked view of database)...............................34

Back to our steps…..*34*

Adding data / rows...*35*

    Add our first recipe 36

    Create a template 38

    Add recipe using the template 40

    Create a new view 40

Summary...*42*

Chapter 4 – Make a travel/holiday planner and learn templates 43

What we are creating..*43*

Create the structure *44*

Creating trip overview database *46*

Add a version *47*

Planning the holiday page setup *48*

Getting ready to go - setup *49*

Trip overview setup..*50*

While on holiday setup *52*

Actions on holiday setup...*56*

Post-holiday reflection setup *57*

Making all of these into a repeatable duplicate *58*

Summary...*59*

Part 3: *60*

Chapter 5 – Connecting databases with a Personal Productivity Management System 61

Getting Things Done (GTD) System 61

What is a Project (within a Productivity system) 62

The PARA System 63

Creating our "Thrive" Productivity System/Tool 64

Initial Task Database Setup 65

Initial Project Database Setup 66

Create our Area Database 72

Creating Database Templates 75

My Home Area example 78

Recurring tasks 80

Summary 80

Chapter 6 – Bringing it all together with dashboards 81

What is a dashboard 81

"Today" Dashboard 82

   Set the layout 82

   Insights Database 83

Thrive Dashboard 96

Summary 108

Summary 109

References 110

Top tips 110

   Create new page: 110

   Move blocks around: 110

   Toggle Sidebar: 110

   Search: 110

Add Comment:	110
Block types:	*110*
Database data types:	*111*
Overview of Synced Blocks	*112*
How to Create Synced Blocks	113
Expanding Synced Blocks	113
Practical Uses of Synced Blocks	113
Tips for Using Synced Blocks	113
Limitations	114
Advanced Tips	114
Books mentioned in this book	*114*
Other book recommendations	*115*
About the author	***116***

Preface

What will I learn in this book and what do I need to know before hand?

"You don't have to see the whole staircase, just take the first step."

Martin Luther King Jr., civil rights leader

About this book

Welcome to Master Notion: break the cycle by creating your own productivity tools. I hope that whether you are new to Notion or dabbled a little bit you find this book useful.

This book is intended to take you on a fun, hands-on journey, to learn how to use Notion. In doing so, you will implement a powerful personal to-do list system that will help you be even more productive in work and life. In each chapter, you will create a tangible, usable system, or tool. The journey will be explained step-by-step and with very little time and effort you will be progressing through. I don't want to waste your time, so we get stuck in straight away from chapter 2. I will cover only areas that you need, but in doing so give you the skills to create with Notion ideas of your own.

> The goal of this book is to teach you how to use Notion, but almost more importantly give you a system that makes you more productive.

So, what will we cover in this book....

Part 1: Context and basics

Chapter 1 – Introduction to **Notion** and how to set it up.
Chapter 2 – Working with blocks by building a **reference area.**

Part 2: Building our first apps with databases

Chapter 3 – Creating a database table, with views for a **personal recipe repertoire.**
Chapter 4 – Make a template for a **travel planner.**

Part 3: Build a personal task management system

Chapter 5 – <u>Connecting databases</u> with a **Personal Task Management System**
Chapter 6 – **Bring it all together** with <u>dashboards</u>.

Requirements

No prior knowledge of productivity methods or tools are needed. Nor do you need any coding or application configuration knowledge.

Notion can look simple at first and then become very daunting, very quickly. We will remove the latter fear.

Each chapter is set-up so that you learn whilst building a tangible tool. Feel free to skip chapters if you know the subjects.

At the relevant places we will go deeper into productivity subjects giving you enough knowledge to understand and be dangerous in the topic.

Contact Information

Contact me at support@infinitypublishing,co.uk with any comments, suggestions, or questions.

Disclaimer

I am not affiliated with Notion at all. I am just a fan and a productivity geek who has finally found a tool that covers a lot of my needs and I want to share this with you all.

Part 1:
Context and basics

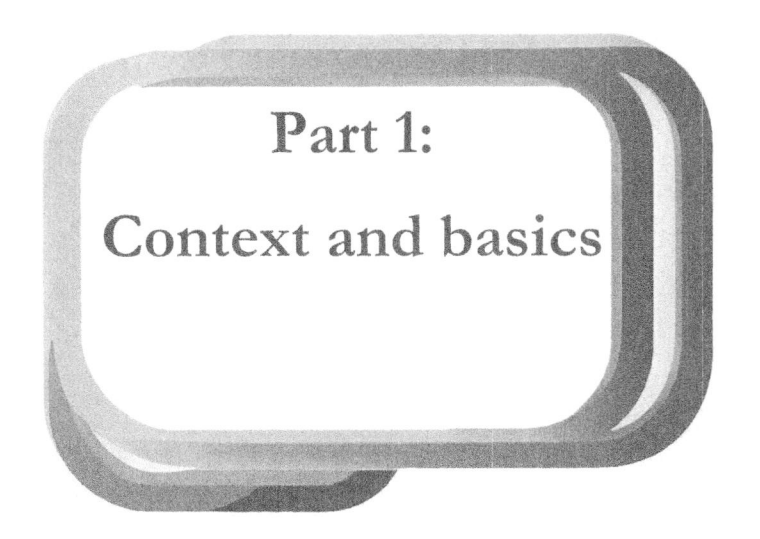

Chapter 1: Introduction to Notion and how to set it up.

Notion is easy to use, and it does a lot more than you probably expect.

"The secret of getting ahead is getting started."

Mark Twain, author, and humorist

> Areas covered in this chapter:
> - What is Notion
> - Install and clear your workspace
> - Create a page

I am so excited that you are about to learn how to harness an amazing, free application - Notion; whilst making (what I hope) will be very useful productivity tools. With this book you will go from thinking Notion is just a note taking tool to realizing its power and what you can achieve with it. Along the way you will learn some productivity tips too and I will point you in the right direction if you want to go deeper into these subjects. My main goal is that you thoroughly enjoy this book and get value from it.

Working through this book

This book is broken down into 6 chapters, where each chapter builds on the skills from the previous. From chapter 2, you will make a different, tangible productivity "tool" each chapter. This is a practical hands-on approach that gets you straight into it. You learn best while doing. If you encounter any problems along the way do drop me a mail at support@infinitypublishing.co.uk and I will try to answer your query.

What is Notion

If you have heard of Notion you may think of Notion as just another note-taking tool, but it offers so much more. Maybe you have heard of Notion and are aware that it's a versatile tool and you want to learn more about it.

At its heart, Notion is a powerful productivity and organization tool that seamlessly combines the functionalities of a to-do list, note-taking platform, and project management software. It allows you to create customizable "databases" that can efficiently store and organize various types of information, such as notes, tasks, ideas, or any set of data you can think of. Notion also offers a range of formatting and media embedding options, making it a versatile tool for creating documents, wikis, and presentations. In addition to its web and mobile apps, Notion also integrates with other popular tools and services, such as Google Calendar and Trello, enabling users to centralize their workflow. Overall, Notion is a powerful and flexible tool that can help individuals and teams increase their productivity and organize their work. In this book we will focus on individual uses only, all using the free, no strings attached version of Notion.

Notion stands out by combining the power of spreadsheets, the flexibility of a text processor, and the organizational capabilities of hierarchical structures all under one roof. In a way, Notion is a low-code platform, i.e. something that with a little configuration can be highly capable.

What can you use Notion for? The possibilities are vast. Here are a few examples:

- A holiday planner
- Recipe book
- Checklist management
- Project and to-do list tracking application
- Budget tracker
- Insurance catalogue
- Customer relationship manager (CRM)
- And much more

Throughout this book, you will learn how to leverage the full potential of Notion to accomplish these tasks and harness its power.

What's truly amazing is that while Notion can serve as a "simple" note-taking application, it also empowers you to develop full-fledged applications without any coding knowledge. In its simplest form, an application consists of an interface, a data store (database), and the ability to hold state. Notion allows you to do all this, and this is exactly what you will learn in this book.

Installing Notion

Installing and configuring Notion on either Mac or PC is really easy.

For Mac, simply visit the App Store and download the Notion app or visit; https://www.notion.so/

For Windows PC, you can go to the same website as above to download the desktop version.

Once you've downloaded and installed the app, open it and then create your account. You can do this either with your email address or by using an Apple or Google account. Please remember to have a strong password as when we are finished Notion may have a lot of your personal information. Remember to **select personal use**, as this is the free account, and you can always upgrade later if you want to.

Get clear and ready

Once installed and open, if you look at the left column, you will see that there are some pre-made pages that Notion provides you, see the image at the top of the next page. All of these are useful, and you can explore them yourself. We will cover the types of functionalities that they all do and so much more. So, for now let's file them away.

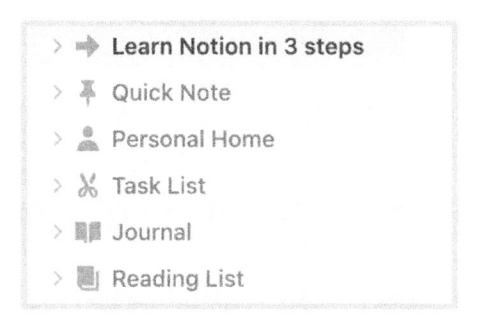

> ➡ **Learn Notion in 3 steps**
> 📌 Quick Note
> 👤 Personal Home
> ✂ Task List
> 📓 Journal
> 📕 Reading List

Notion pages can contain other pages, this is one of many powerful features in Notion. So, let's create a page and drag all these pre-made files into it for later.

1. Click the New page button in the left column.

   ⊕ New page
   > 📄 Original Templates

2. In the title section choose something like "Original Templates". The name can be anything, it doesn't matter.

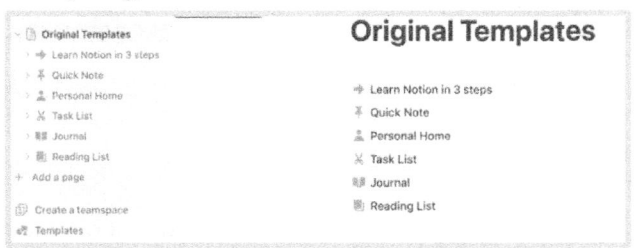

   # Original Templates

   ➡ Learn Notion in 3 steps
   📌 Quick Note
   👤 Personal Home
   ✂ Task List
   📓 Journal
   📕 Reading List

3. Drag all the pre-made pages into the "Original Templates" page. Don't worry they won't get deleted. In fact, you will see original templates becomes an expandable list, see the two images below. The pages also become links within Original Templates, see the images below.

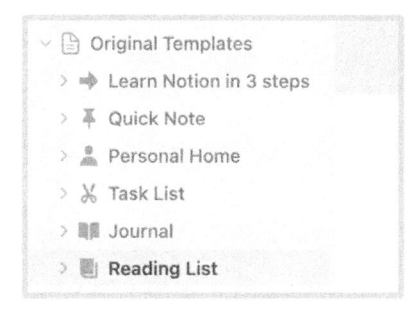

   ∨ 📄 Original Templates
   > ➡ Learn Notion in 3 steps
   > 📌 Quick Note
   > 👤 Personal Home
   > ✂ Task List
   > 📓 Journal
   > 📕 **Reading List**

1: Introduction

Chapter Summary

First chapter done. Easy right?

We have learnt a little bit about Notion. Installed it and cleared away the initial clutter.

We even created our first page. In the next chapter, we will learn about Notion's key features and start building a useful tool/page.

As we dive into the next five chapters, we will explore the vast array of key features that Notion has to offer. These features will empower you to build efficient and practical tools to enhance your workflow. Get ready to unlock the full potential of Notion as we embark on a journey of discovery and creation.

In the upcoming chapter, you can expect to:

1. Gain in-depth knowledge about the various key features of Notion.
2. Explore how these features can be utilized to build personalized and powerful tools.
3. Learn advanced techniques to optimize your productivity within Notion.
4. Engage in hands-on exercises and practical examples to reinforce your understanding.

As we progress through this book, your proficiency with Notion will steadily grow, allowing you to leverage its capabilities to their fullest extent. So, buckle up and get ready for an exciting chapter filled with valuable insights and practical applications. We are now ready to up the pace and learn and create more.

Chapter 2 – Working with blocks by building a Reference Area and Today focused Task Management Page

Blocks are literally the building blocks of any Notion page.

"To be prepared is half the victory."

Miguel de Cervantes, author

> Areas covered in this chapter:
> - Blocks
> - Embed a page within a page
> - Link to a page
> - Rollups
> - Dividers
> - Basic tables
> - Columns

Let's get straight into it and create our first (proper) Notion pages by creating a personal reference area.

What exactly do I mean by reference area? Think of it as a second brain - a space to group and store things you want or need to remember. The way we group these items isn't crucial because Notion offers strong search capabilities. However, logically organizing them will enhance the visual experience when working in this area.

> **TIP: Second brain:** A second brain is a concept in productivity and organization that refers to a system or method for storing and organizing information outside of one's own mind, to free up mental space. This can take many forms, such as a simple note-taking system

or a digital database, an app. The idea is to have a reliable and accessible way to offload information and ideas, allowing you to focus on the task at hand and easily retrieve information when needed. Notion is a popular tool for creating a second brain, as it allows for flexible and customizable organization of information in various formats. The key here is to get it out of your head into a reliable place, so you aren't making efforts to remember something.

This reference page will be deliberately simple. We'll avoid using some of Notion's powerful features for now, which we'll cover later. Once we've learned those features, you can return to this page and enhance it. Nevertheless, this page will still be useful and serve as a solid foundation for learning the basics of Notion's features.

Before we create the page, let's briefly learn about blocks.

What are Notion blocks?

Notion blocks are an incredibly powerful concept that are used to organize your thoughts and tasks in a simple and efficient manner.

What is important, amazing and one of Notion's most powerful features is that any block can be transformed into any of the different block types. E.g. turn a heading into a page or bullet point or then to a to-do.

In this guide, I will provide an overview of the types of blocks available and how to use them to their fullest potential.

Notion's block system is versatile and allows you to create and organize content in a modular way. The different types of blocks are described below.

Text Blocks

The most basic Notion block is the Text block, which is used for simple text input. You can use Text blocks for headings, paragraphs, and lists. Notion also supports Markdown syntax, so you can format your text using headings, bold, italics, and other styles.

Within this you can do:

Quote Blocks

Quote blocks are used to highlight a specific quote or passage from a text. This is particularly useful for keeping track of important information or ideas that you want to reference later.

Callout Blocks

Callout blocks are used to draw attention to specific information within a page. They are like Quote blocks but are typically used for shorter pieces of information, like a warning or a note.

Other block types can be found in References.

When you create a block, it can be easily moved around by clicking the six dots, see the image below. You can move blocks up or down, and in some cases, you can even place them within or to the left/right of other blocks. We'll cover this in more detail later when we create columns in our Today dashboard.

Building a Reference Page (Create a Notion page)

So, let's create our first page. This will be the simple references page; well in fact it will be a collection of pages. Everything in this will be searchable, so it's a great place to organize and store things in a logical way. As we said this could be done in a more complicated, feature rich way, but we need to start somewhere.

1. To create a new page open Notion and click the + New Page button in the top left, see below.

2: Working with Blocks

2. Click the 3 dots in the top right of the window, see below and turn on *small* text and *full width*. We will be doing this for every page throughout this book.

3. Select *Empty page* from below. Later, we can create templates that we can use instead, or you can select a pre-made Notion template.

4. Let's give our page the title: "References".

5. Now to make the page look better; in both the left-hand task bar and within the page itself let's give it an icon. Select the *Add icon* option above our new title - see below.

References

6. Select an icon. You have three options 1) a colorful emoji, 2) a set of icons built into Notion (when you choose one you can select its color) and 3) you can upload your own or provide a weblink.

7. Also, to make it look good, let's add a cover. Click *Add cover*, next to the *Add icon* option. A random cover will be automatically added. I like to use either a plain color or an image that goes with the page's theme. In this case let's select an image, and move it to where we like:

    7.1) Move the mouse over the cover and select *Change* cover

    7.2) You will see different options:

    - Notion's own images (the first set are what I use for plain colors)
    - Option to upload your own.
    - Use a web link to an image.
    - Or Unsplash, an external, free image library

    Select *Unsplash* and search for something that you like; in this case I used "library".

    7.3) Hover over the cover again and choose *Reposition*. You can then move it up or down to where you like. See my result below using the image I selected.

    References

8. Now, let's build out the main body of the page. Click in the main page and type ">" and double space, this will create a *Toggle list*. A toggle list is a block type that can be opened and closed by clicking the triangle to the left. In bold type "Rules for life and work". This is what you will always see whether the list is expanded or not.

9. With the toggle open type, the following numbered list. Note you can always drag things in and out of a toggle list.

2: Working with Blocks

1. Never take a break on impulse
2. Never put paper back into a pile without an associate action
3. Think of three things each morning that you are grateful for, then decide what you will achieve that day.

10. Let's change the color of this block by clicking on the 6 dots to the left and select Color, see image below and choose a background color of green. There are not loads of color options in Notion as the developers are trying to keep the product as simple as possible.

    Color

11. Add a divider by clicking the plus and selecting *Divider*. You can also do this by typing a double "-".

12. Now, let's embed a page within this References page.

12.1) We will give it a header, type "/heading 2" and type "Things to remember by area:", hit enter

12.2) Type "/page". This will create a new page. The title of the page will be the name seen in **References**. To match the example, recreate the below image yourself.

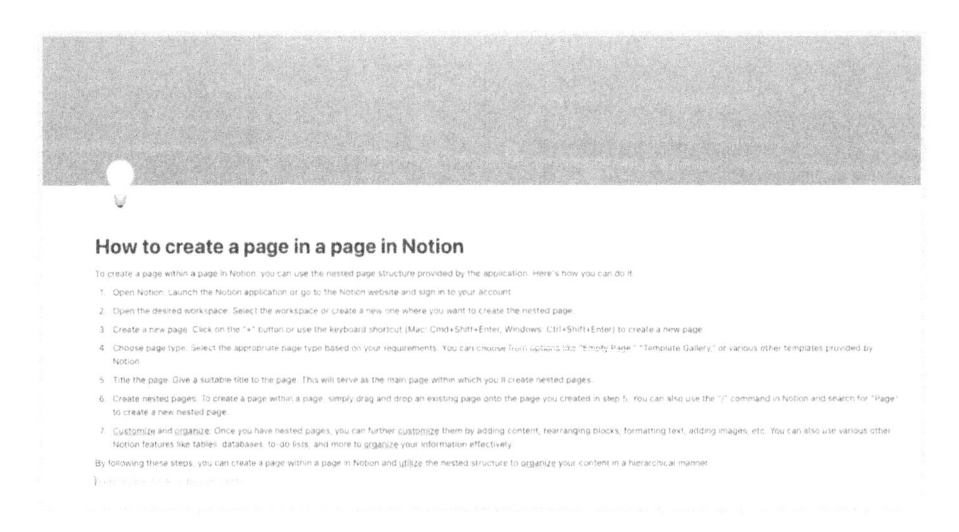

How to create a page in a page in Notion

After creating the page, you will notice that you can expand out References and see the new embedded page. You can embed as many pages to as many layers

22

as you would like. Think of it like a folder structure in your computer - a great way to organize different information items.

Once completed your page should look like the image below. Hopefully already, through this first simple example you are starting to get a sense of the flexibility and power of Notion.

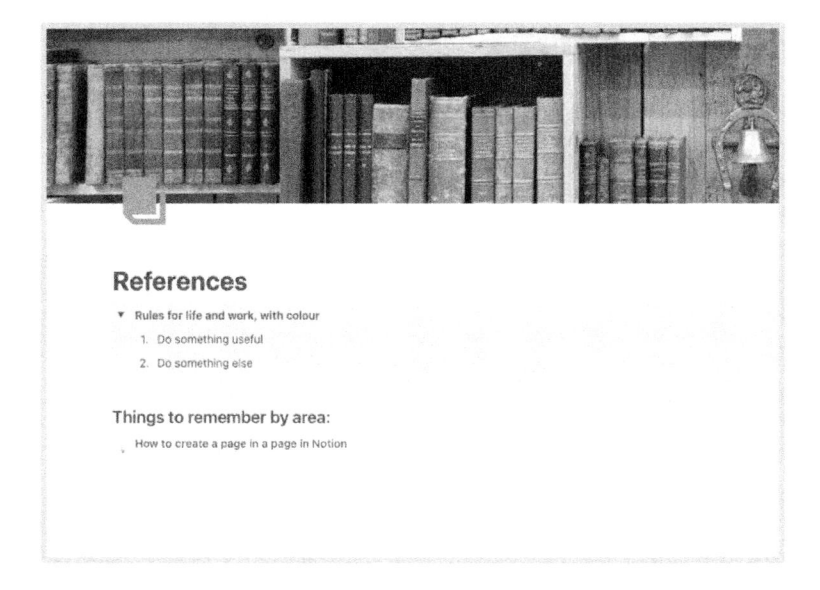

Searchability: I mentioned this earlier and it's worth re-highlighting the point. This page/content and anything in Notion is searchable. The search feature in Notion is a powerful tool that enables users to swiftly navigate through their vast collection of notes, documents, and databases (we will come to these later) with remarkable efficiency.

With its robust search capabilities, Notion empowers users to quickly locate specific information, saving them valuable time and enhancing their productivity. The search feature in Notion goes beyond basic keyword matching, as it intelligently considers the context and relevance of the searched terms. It can effortlessly retrieve results from various file types, including text, images, PDFs, and more.

Additionally, the search feature offers advanced filtering options, allowing users to narrow down their search results based on specific criteria, such as tags, dates, or file types. Whether users are seeking a specific paragraph within a lengthy document or trying to locate a specific database entry, Notion's search feature delivers accurate and swift results, making it an indispensable tool for organizing and retrieving information effectively.

Building a "Today" Dashboard (Create a Notion page, with links to others)

The Today Dashboard will be (in Chapter 6) the most important part of our whole productivity system. Why is it so important? We can only do a task in the now, everything else is just planning and the power is knowing what the right thing to do is, at the right time and in the right context/place. This dashboard gives you the information you need for now, it's your job to do the task and get it done. For now, we will make a basic, but useful version of what we will enhance later.

1. Create a new page as before in the previous step 1 and 2, make sure you:

1.1) Set the page to small text and full width
1.2) Give it an icon, I went with a red target - see below.

2. Create another new page, same as above but call it ">> Inbox" and give it an icon and cover like below.

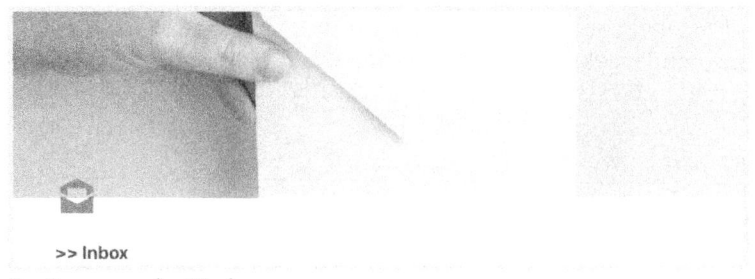

>> Inbox

3. Re-open the Today page.
4. We will create a link to the >> Inbox page by typing /Link to page and selecting >> Inbox. A linked page is not within the structure of the page

calling it and therefore can be linked to from multiple pages. This is good when you want that page to be a stand-alone page.

> **TIP: Inbox:** The Inbox page in Notion serves as a versatile tool for capturing your thoughts, ideas, and actions in a centralized location. It acts as a digital "inbox" where you can quickly jot down and organize your notes, tasks, and reminders. Here's how you can effectively use the Inbox page in Notion:
>
> 1. **Capture spontaneous thoughts**: Whenever an idea or thought strikes you, simply open the Notion app or webpage and navigate to your Inbox page. Write down your thoughts as brief notes, bullet points, or paragraphs. Don't worry about formatting or organization at this stage; the primary focus is on capturing ideas as they come to mind.
> 2. **Create to-do items**: If you have tasks or actions that need to be completed, turn them into actionable to-do items in your Inbox. For each task, include a clear description and any relevant details. You can use checkboxes to mark tasks as complete once they are finished.
> 3. **Add context and categorization**: To better organize your thoughts and actions, consider adding additional context to each entry in the Inbox. You can include tags, labels, due dates, or priority levels to provide further context and facilitate later sorting or filtering. This will help you easily locate and prioritize tasks when you're ready to address them.
> 4. **Regularly review and process**: Set aside regular intervals to review your Inbox page. During this review process, evaluate each entry and decide what action needs to be taken. You can categorize tasks as "Do Now," "Delegate," "Schedule," or "Defer" based on their urgency and importance. Take the time to assign tasks to specific projects or move them to appropriate pages within Notion for further action.
> 5. **Organize and categorize**: Once you have processed your Inbox entries, it's essential to organize and categorize them properly. Create dedicated pages or databases within Notion to house related projects, tasks, or ideas. Move the relevant entries from the

2: Working with Blocks

> Inbox to their respective locations, maintaining a clean and organized workspace.
> 6. **Maintain an empty Inbox**: The ultimate goal is to keep your Inbox page clear and empty. Regularly process and transfer your captured thoughts and actions to appropriate pages or databases, ensuring that nothing gets overlooked. Strive for a clutter-free Inbox that represents only new and unprocessed items.
>
> By leveraging the power of the Inbox page in Notion, you can streamline your thought-capturing process, prevent information overload, and stay organized. It acts as a reliable starting point for all your ideas and tasks, allowing you to transform them into actionable items and seamlessly integrate them into your overall productivity workflow.

5. Next let's add our first call out. In Notion, a callout is a formatting feature used to draw attention to specific information or highlight important details within a page. It is essentially a stylized box or container that stands out from the rest of the content. We will also use these later to create certain styles within a page. Callouts can be useful for various purposes, such as emphasizing key points, providing additional context, creating visual breaks in the content, or simply making important information more noticeable. Notion offers different callout styles and customization options, allowing you to adapt them to your specific needs and preferences such as changing the background color or associated icon. To create a call out, add a line by hitting the + or hit enter and type "/callout".

6. Choose an icon and type "Goal of the day: Complete a new Notion page." It should look like the image below.

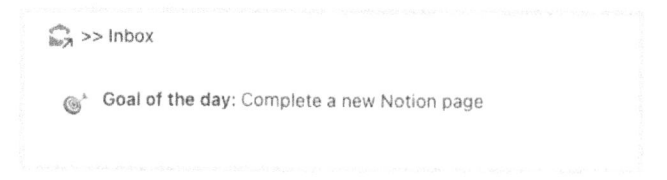

>> Inbox

◎ **Goal of the day**: Complete a new Notion page

7. Let's add our first layout feature. We will add three columns - columns allow you to organize content side by side, like how you would arrange information in a table or spreadsheet. By using columns, you can create a multi-column structure within a page or document, which helps in presenting data or content in a more structured and visually appealing way.

Columns in Notion are flexible, and you can even have a different number of columns in each column block. Let's add 3 columns underneath our call out by typing "/3 columns". Once created they are hard to see unless you change their background color.

8. *Left-click* the + button and add a *heading 2* called "Today".

9. *Left-click* on the 6-dots and choose *Color→Red background*.

10. *Left-click* and hold on the 6-dots and drag the Today heading into the left column. You can see the column borders flash with blue on the left. If done correctly it should look like the image below. Note the reduced width.

Today
Press 'space' for AI, '/' for commands

11. Create a *heading 2* called "Tomorrow" and *left-click* on the 6-dots and choose *Color→Yellow background*.

12. *Left-click* and hold on the 6-dots and drag the Tomorrow heading into the rightmost column, leaving the middle free. You can see the column borders flash with blue on the left. If done correctly it should look like the image below.

Today		Tomorrow
Press 'space' for AI, '/' for commands		

13. Click the + button and create a table by typing "/table". *Left-click* and hold on the 6-dots and drag the table into the middle column. By default, you get a two column, 3 row table. You can add columns by clicking the grey + button to the right of the column, see the image below or add a row by doing the same below a row.

14. We are going to use the table to create a simple diary view of the day. Complete it to look like the below image.

```
Before 08:00

08:00: 09:00

09:00: 10:00

10:00: 11:00

11:00: 12:00

12:00: 13:00

13:00: 14:00

14:00: 15:00

15:00: 16:00

16:00: 17:00

17:00: 18:00

Evening
```

15. Let's add a to-do element below each of our headings in columns. In Notion, a to-do element is a task management feature that helps you keep track of your tasks, prioritize them, and mark them as complete. Click + in each column and type "/to-do list". Re-create the below image. You will note a call out there too.

16. Finally, let's add a scratch pad area for random notes and thoughts in the day under the columns. Create a *heading 2* called "Scratch pad" with a grey background color and add some text below. When done your new page should look the image below when completed.

Chapter Summary

Remember, we will come back to the Today dashboard later and make significant improvements once we have created a full life/work area, project, and task management system.

Next chapter we will really start unlocking the power of Notion by building our first database. Hopefully this chapter has given you a great taster for what Notion can do and even these two simple pages can be of use. We have got used to creating pages and adding elements to those pages to conceptually create useful pages that are linked together. Next, we are going to learn about arguably Notion's most powerful feature - databases.

Part 2:
Building our first apps with databases

Chapter 3 – Creating a database, with templates and different views for a personal recipe repertoire.

Build your own stand-alone digital recipe book.

"Eating is a necessity, but cooking is an art."

Anonymous

> Areas covered in this chapter:
> - Create a database.
> - Manage views of a database.
> - Create a database template.

We have seen how flexible a Notion page can be by using blocks. Let's look deeper into the most powerful block type – the **database table.** A table is of course a set of rows and columns to contain data; and basic tables can be added into Notion as a block. What makes Notion different is that in a database table, it still contains rows and columns, but each row can be a Notion page on its own and can contain whatever blocks you want. You can also change the view of the database table very easily – more on this later in this chapter.

In later chapters we will learn how to connect tables and turn them into basic applications/databases, but let's start with creating a useful personal recipe repertoire "system" with a single table.

Let's create a recipe repertoire/book in Notion. If you're someone who loves to cook or bake, you probably have a collection of recipes that you've gathered over the years from various magazines, shops, and people. Instead of keeping

4: Travel Planner

them all in a messy pile or scattered across various platforms, why not create a recipe book in Notion? Well, that's what we are about to do.

How to create:

1. Create a new page.

2. Give the page a title, an icon and cover picture, I went with the below.

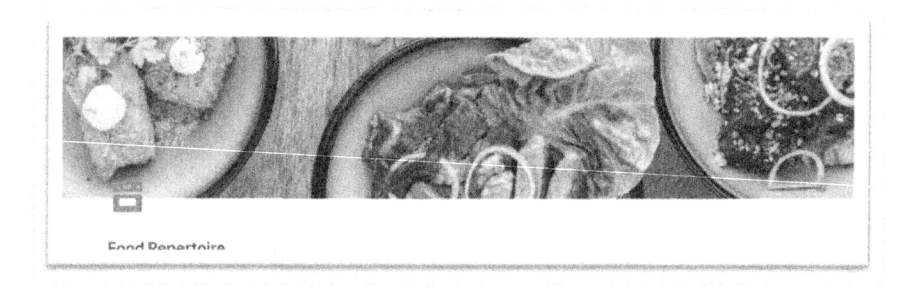

[Image: Food Repertoire page header with food photo]

3. As per the previous chapter, click the 3 dots and set **Small text** on and **Full width** on.

4. Add a **Database-inline** block or use the shortcut "/data " and you will see this option.

Small, important tangent on Databases within Notion

When adding a database into Notion you will see the following options:

- Database – Inline
- Database – Full page
- Table view
- Board view
- Gallery view
- List view
- Calendar view
- Timeline view
- Linked view of a database

The first two are Databases, displayed in different ways - (inline is within a page and full page creates a new page) the rest are **views**. Views are different ways to view the same data stored within a Database table to suit your needs. Even

3: Databases & Recipe Book

after selecting a pre-set view, you can configure it how you want. You can also switch the view later too. Let's take a moment to understand each of the views below - within each title I have included the shortcut.

Table View (/table view)

The table view is the default view for Notion databases. It displays the data in a traditional table format, with columns and rows. You can customize the columns to show the data you want, and you can sort and filter the data by clicking on the column headers. This view is great for organizing data that is best displayed in a table format, such as a calendar or task list.

Board View (/board view)

The board view displays the data in a visual card format, like Trello. Each card represents a record in the database, and you can customize the fields displayed on the cards. You can drag and drop the cards to rearrange them, and you can group them by any field. This view is great for organizing data that has a visual component, such as project management or brainstorming.

Gallery View (/gallery view)

The gallery view displays the data in a visual gallery format, with each record displayed as a card. You can customize the fields displayed on the cards, and you can group the cards by any field. This view is great for organizing data that has a visual component, such as images or design inspiration.

List View (/list view)

The list view displays the data in a vertical list format, with each record displayed as a row. You can customize the fields displayed in the list, and you can sort and filter the data by clicking on the column headers. This view is great for organizing data that is best displayed in a list format, such as a contact list or inventory.

Calendar View (/calendar view)

The calendar view displays the data in a monthly calendar format, with each record displayed as an event. You can customize the fields displayed on the calendar, and you can drag and drop events to rearrange them. You can also create recurring events, set reminders, and invite guests to events. This view is great for organizing data that has a date component, such as a schedule or appointments.

Timeline View (/timeline view)

The timeline view displays the data in a Gannt chart or more commonly known as a plan.

4: Travel Planner

Linked view of a database (/linked view of database)

The linked view of a database gives you a synchronized copy of the same content from another database - we will cover this more in Chapter 5.

Notion offers this variety of database views to suit different needs to organize and view data. Each view has its own unique features and benefits, and as stated earlier, you can switch between views easily to find the one that works best for you or the situation.

Back to our steps...

Having selected a Database-inline block you should have a default table as below.

⊞ Table		
Untitled		
Aa Name	Tags	...
+ New		

Let's spend a moment understanding what we have here. The core of all databases is the table. This table has two columns or fields - Name and Tags. These are the default and can be changed. A column can be of different types. In this case *Name* is text and this column is what's called a primary key - the main reference for any grouping of data. You can change the name of the *Name* column, but not the type. At the time of writing this must be text based. I do hope Notion allows this to be a number as well in the future. The other column is *Tags* and this is a multi-select type. This column can be deleted or changed. A row in this table will be our grouping of data.

As mentioned above we can change how we view this table, but the easiest way to set-up a database in my view is via the table view.

So, let's configure our table.

5. First let's give the database a name. Click *Untitled* and give it a name, I have gone with *The Carr recipe book*.

6. Change *Name* to *Recipe*

3: Databases & Recipe Book

7. Right-click on *Tags*, select *Edit property*, see below. Click *Tags* and rename to *Ingredients*. We will leave this as a multi-select type. This means, we can select a few options. Let's create some (you can add more later as you and when you add recipes).

   a. Click *Add an option* and type *Garlic*
   b. Hit enter and you will see it appear with a random color (you can change the color later)
   c. Click the + button and type Rice, hit enter.
   d. Close that box, by pressing the x

8. Let's get back to adding columns. This time click the + to the right of Ingredients.

9. In the box, lets add the name *Chef*, then click *Text* in the Type list.

10. Repeat adding columns for the following:

    a. Add Type and make it of Type Multi-select
    b. Add Serves and make it of Type Number
    c. Add Pre time and make it of Type Number
    d. Add Cook time and make it of Type Number

11. Now we are going to add a special and powerful Type, one that Excel users will be partially familiar with - a function.

    a. Add a new column as usual and call it *Total time*. This time select Type *Formula*.
    b. In the Edit space type the following formula:
       ```
       prop("Prep time") + prop("Cook time")
       ```

Here we are simply adding the number in the *Prep time* column to the number in the *Cook time* row by referring to the columns within the *prop("") function*. There are many more functions that we will cover later in this book.

Adding data / rows

That's it, we have set up the database ready for our recipes. Let's add two recipes and then we are going to change how the recipes are viewed. First, we will add a recipe, then we will create a template and use that to create the next.

4: Travel Planner

Add our first recipe

Let's create our first recipe. For this, I will give you one of my own - Car-bron-ara, my take and enhancement of a traditional Carbonara.

12. Click the blue New button, see below. This will come up with an input form, based on the columns we added in the last piece. Another way of looking at this form is that it is a page within Notion. So, you can do or add anything into this page, including another database! We are going to add the detailed ingredients and method into the text/page area itself.

13. Add the details as per the screenshot below. Remember *Total* time will automatically be calculated.

> **Note: Add a property:** If you add something here it will add a column to the database, and this will apply to all future rows/data items.

3: Databases & Recipe Book

Car-bron-ara

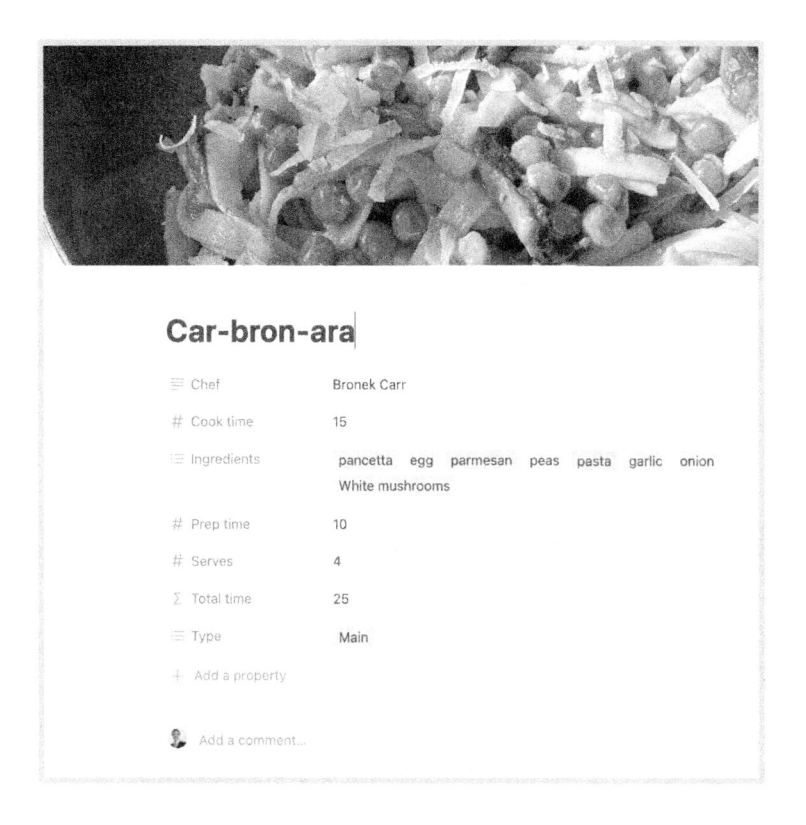

≡ Chef	Bronek Carr
# Cook time	15
≡ Ingredients	pancetta egg parmesan peas pasta garlic onion White mushrooms
# Prep time	10
# Serves	4
∑ Total time	25
≡ Type	Main
+ Add a property	

👤 Add a comment...

14. Let's add the ingredients and the method. In the main part of the page, select *Empty page*. Then start by adding a *Toggle list*. Type **Ingredients**. Anything within the toggle list can be hidden or expanded by opening it up. I use this to hide the ingredients to focus on the cooking method.

15. Add the ingredients in a *Bulleted list* as per the image below.

16. Then add a *Heading 2*. Type Method and in a *Numbered list* add the details below.

37

17. Later you can add a cover photo of the food itself, this will help when we create a new view of the database later in this chapter.

> ▼ **Ingredients**
> - 2 packets (200g) - pancetta
> - 4 eggs - 3 full eggs + 1 yoke
> - 50 grams - grated parmesan cheese
> - 175 grams - frozen peas
> - 2 closes - garlic
> - Half - White onion
> - 300g - White Mushrooms
> - 500g - Fresh Tagliatelle pasta
>
> **Method**
> 1. Crisp pancetta, remove
> 2. Cook onion in (half)
> 3. Garlic and mushrooms, add peas and pancetta
> 4. Add salt and pepper
> 5. Add boiled pasta
> 6. Stir in egg and 75% cheese

No need to hit save; just close the page or go back and you will see a row has been added to the table and that you have created your first recipe.

Create a template

Let's make it easier to add recipes in future. You can do this by creating a *Template*.

In Notion, a template refers to a pre-designed and pre-structured layout or framework that can be used as a starting point for creating new pages or databases.

Templates can be created by yourself or obtained from the Notion Template Gallery, which offers a wide range of ready-made templates. Once you have completed this book you will understand how these templates can be changed and even create your own for other people. When you create a new page or database in Notion, you have the option to start with a blank canvas or choose from a selection of templates.

To make a template:

1) Click the down arrow next to the blue *New* button

2) Select + *New Template*

3: Databases & Recipe Book

3) Add details to the page as per below. The template will be named after the page title.

You will note I haven't completed any of the data items from the column

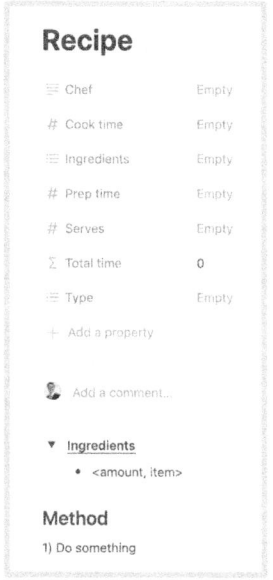

```
Recipe
  Chef            Empty
  Cook time       Empty
  Ingredients     Empty
  Prep time       Empty
  Serves          Empty
  Total time      0
  Type            Empty
  + Add a property

  Add a comment...

  ▼ Ingredients
      • <amount, item>

  Method
  1) Do something
```

headers/fields. You can, but in this case, I expect them to change in each recipe.

4) Close the window or go back.

Remember, this is a template only, so we haven't added a row into our Food Repertoire.

5) The final step is to make this new template our default when we create new recipes.

5.1) Click the down arrow near new again.

5.2) Click the ... next to *Recipe* and choose *Set as default*

It should now look like the image below. Personally, I keep the empty page option, but you can remove this.

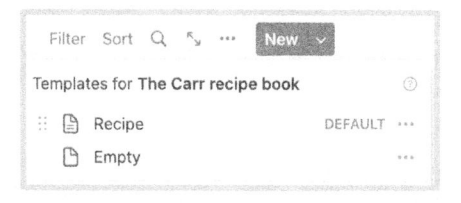

```
Filter  Sort  Q  ⤴  ···    New  ⌄
Templates for The Carr recipe book           ⓘ
  ⋮⋮  📄  Recipe              DEFAULT  ···
      📄  Empty                        ···
```

39

4: Travel Planner

Add recipe using the template

Let's use our new template to create a new template. Again, I will give you one of my own recipes. This is a dressing recipe I got from a chain of restaurants in London called Humble Grape. We loved it so much I asked the staff for it. It's superb on salad greens such as rocket or lamb lettuce but can be used with all sorts.

1) Click the blue New button. This time you will see its pre-populated with our recipe template as we made it default. You can also use the down arrow to select a different template if you wish.

2) Fill in the details below, again add a cover picture if you wish, this will make it look better when we create a different view next.

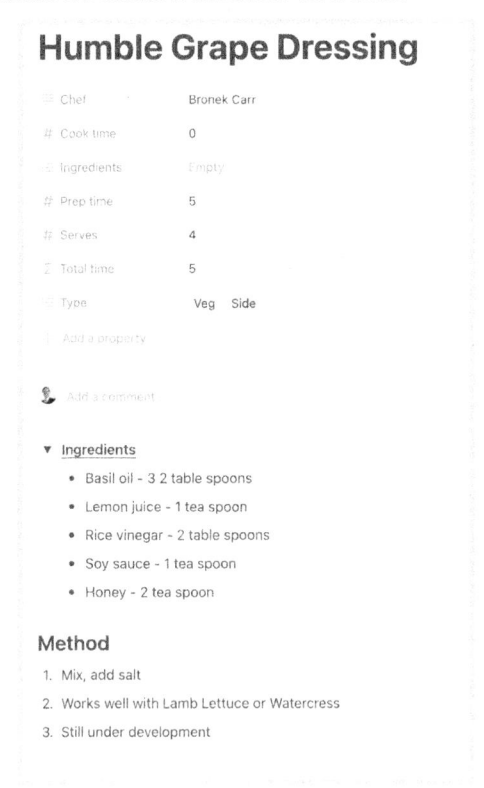

Humble Grape Dressing

Chef	Bronek Carr
Cook time	0
Ingredients	Empty
Prep time	5
Serves	4
Total time	5
Type	Veg Side

Add a property

Add a comment

▼ Ingredients
- Basil oil - 3 2 table spoons
- Lemon juice - 1 tea spoon
- Rice vinegar - 2 table spoons
- Soy sauce - 1 tea spoon
- Honey - 2 tea spoon

Method
1. Mix, add salt
2. Works well with Lamb Lettuce or Watercress
3. Still under development

Create a new view

As we discussed earlier you can change the view of a Notion database easily. Our default was the table view. For everyday use the *Gallery view i*s much better.

40

3: Databases & Recipe Book

Rather than change the table view, we will create a new view, so that we have both a table and a gallery view to select. To do this:

1) Click the + next to *Table view* - see the image below.

2) Choose *Gallery view*. I will name it *"Gallery"*, but you can call it what you want.

3) In *Card preview*, select *Page cover*. This will show the images that we add to the page/recipe covers and make it look more appealing. See below.

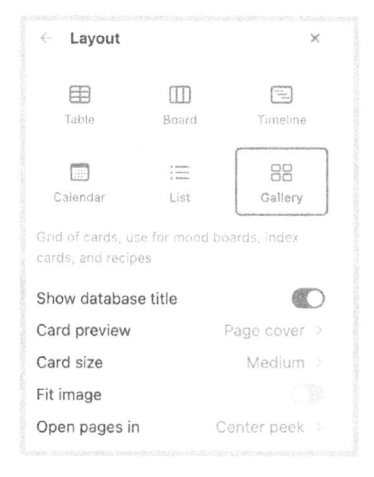

4) Select Properties and choose which data items you want to be hidden from the gallery "thumbnail". I went with those below.

4: Travel Planner

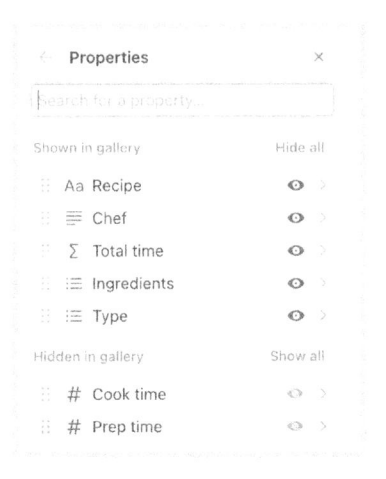

And that's it. It should look something like the below. You can now click the *Gallery view* and *Table view* to switch the display of the recipe data.

Summary

Hopefully this chapter has given you a great experience of how to create and use databases in Notion. I hope even more that you find the recipes and the system itself useful to get rid of all those magazine cutouts or random bookmarked links that you have. This is just a single standalone database - when we link multiple databases in later chapters you see even more possibilities. These databases are searchable, or you can filter tables on specific items. This means if you have specific ingredients in the cupboard, you might find a recipe that will inspire you, or find something you can do on Vegan night.

Chapter 4 – Make a travel/holiday planner and learn templates

Build your own re-usable travel planner.

"The journey itself is my home."

Matsuo Basho, Japanese poet

Areas covered in this chapter:
- Make a set of pages and associated databases repeatable.
- Google maps integration
- Create a menu toolbar

In the previous chapter we learnt how to make a database, with different views. In this chapter we are going to combine our knowledge so far by combining pages and databases into a powerful holiday planner and making this a repeatable template. I should say at this stage that there is a holiday planner template built into Notion, but in this chapter, we are going to make a better one (one that is much nicer looking) and learn whilst doing so.

What we are creating

We are creating a comprehensive travel and trip planner, consisting of a series of pages to assist you in every stage of your journey, from the initial planning phase to the actual trip and even after you return. This versatile planner is suitable for both work and personal trips. Each page, along with the connected databases, contributes to a cohesive mini application. Additionally, we will explore how to iterate and enhance the planner to best suit your needs.

4: Travel Planner

In this example, we will use it for a trip to Greece in January 2024, but the place and time doesn't matter. Once you have the template you can configure it for wherever you want.

Create the structure

For this chapter's example we are going to create multiple pages, with a main page as the "home page". At the end, each page will have an identical menu that gets you to the relevant sub-area. Let's start with creating the blank pages, with the relevant cover photos / icons.

1) Create the main page called "Trip Plan: Greece | January 2024", full width, small text. For the main page I picked a cover photo of the area from *Unsplash*. My blank page looks like the image below.

Trip Plan: Greece | January 2024

2) Create another page called "Planning the holiday", full width, small text. Have just an icon this time. My blank page looks like the below image.

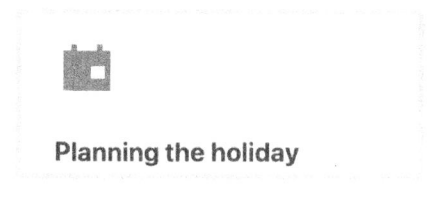

Planning the holiday

3) Drag this page into *Trip Plan: Greece | January 2024* via the left-hand side task bar, like in the image below.

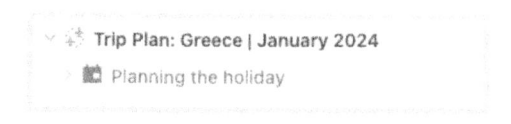

  Trip Plan: Greece | January 2024
    Planning the holiday

4) Repeat steps 2 and 3 to create the pages with icons in the image below.

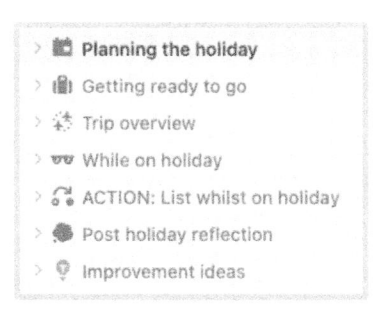

> 📕 Planning the holiday
> 🧳 Getting ready to go
> 🧗 Trip overview
> 👀 While on holiday
> 🎬 ACTION: List whilst on holiday
> 🌍 Post holiday reflection
> 💡 Improvement ideas

That's all the pages we are going to need to interconnect. Let's build each one further.

Complete the "homepage" and menu.

Our home page will have two main elements:

1) A menu; and

2) A trip overview.

Setting up the menu

By creating a menu on the homepage and replicating it on other pages it makes this set of Notion pages feel like an application. To create the menu:

1) Create a callout using "/callout". Callouts are usually used to call out key points in a page, we are going to use it to create a border with an icon that we can contain our menu within. At first the callout will span the whole of the page, but later we will add it to a column.

2) Type "**Menu:**"

3) Click the icon and change it to this image.

🗄 Menu:

4: Travel Planner

4) In the left-hand taskbar, click the 3 dots next to this page "Trip Plan: Greece | January 2024" page and select *Copy link*. Then in the call out hit *shift + enter* after "**Menu:**". Paste the link in and hit enter. You should see the following.

Note: You can drag blocks to a call out, but if you want to explicitly add a new space you must hit *shift + enter* as just enter takes you out of the call out.

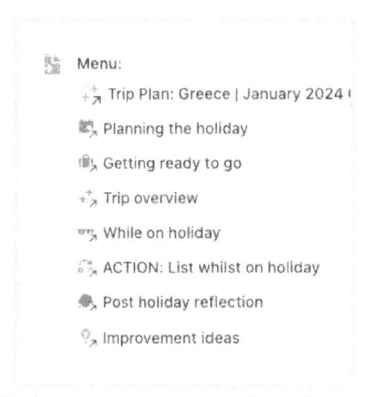

5) Repeat this for all the pages we created in the previous section. By the end your menu should look like the image below.

6) Copy and paste this menu to each of the pages we created in the previous section. We now have a menu that is the same across all pages so we can jump around easily.

Creating trip overview database

We will create an "at a glance" view of when we are going, how long for and the number of days before we go. This is a bit overkill, but the best way of doing this is via a stand-alone database. We will use some more advanced formulas than we did in Chapter 3.

Under the menu do the following.

1) Create an inline database using "/database - inline", keep in the table view and add the following columns:

1.1) "Name", type *text*

46

1.2) "When", type *date*

1.3) "Duration", type formula, with the following formula - "*dateBetween(end(prop("When")), start(prop("When")), "days") + 1*". In this formula we are counting the days between the end and start date added into the *When* column, we then add a day as it doesn't count the first day.

1.4) "Days before we go", type formula, with the following formula - "*dateBetween(start(prop("When")), now(), "days")*". In this formula we are counting the days between now and the first day we go.

I have added the following data to my trip as an example.

Name: "This trip"

When: "1st Jan 2024 - 5th Jan 2025" (remember to select end date when adding this or it would be just one day.

The formula columns will automatically update.

2) Drag the database to the right of our menu.

Add a version

3) Add a divider line below the menu and the database using "*/divider*".

4) Below the line, in *gray* color write "v1.0"

Once done our completed "homepage" should look like this.

4: Travel Planner

That is our first page done.

Planning the holiday page setup

Now we will do a simple holiday planning page. The intent for this page is to capture all the things you need to do to make the holiday happen. As we complete some of these tasks, we will add the details into our *trip overview* page that we will create later.

1) Below the menu create a *h2* "Tasks to book the holiday"

2) Drag this header to the right of the menu, like step 2) in creating the homepage. Press *enter* and it should create a line below, if not you can drag each of the blocks as you create them.

3) Add a /*divider* below the header

4) Then add /*to-do list* blocks as per the below, complete page. Note the links to "Trip overview" to make it easier to add the details. The intent of these to-dos is to capture things you must do to make the trip happen, feel free to add more such as "add hotel loyalty card number to booking".

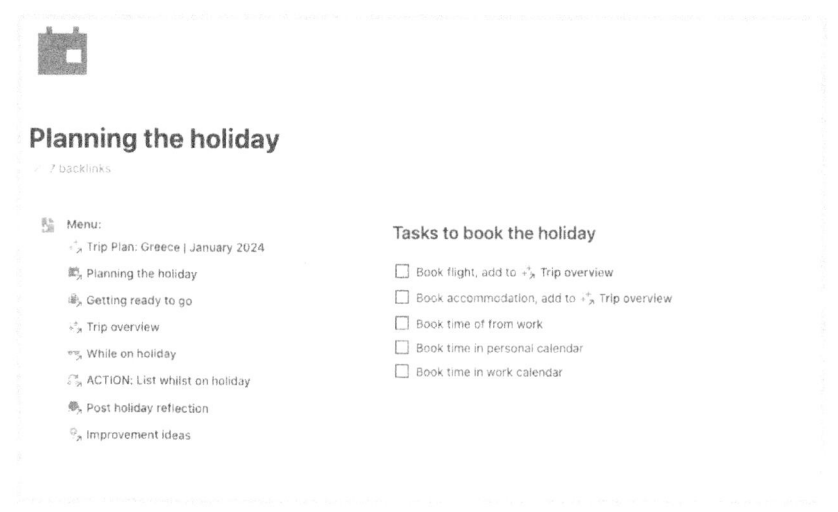

Planning the holiday

7 backlinks

Menu:
- Trip Plan: Greece | January 2024
- Planning the holiday
- Getting ready to go
- Trip overview
- While on holiday
- ACTION: List whilst on holiday
- Post holiday reflection
- Improvement ideas

Tasks to book the holiday
- [ ] Book flight, add to Trip overview
- [ ] Book accommodation, add to Trip overview
- [ ] Book time of from work
- [ ] Book time in personal calendar
- [ ] Book time in work calendar

Note: you should try to match the menu width to the homepage. You can do this by hovering the mouse over the divider line until you see a gray bar like in the image below.

48

Another page done, let's move to the next.

Getting ready to go - setup

The purpose of this page is to use a few days, if not the night before you go to make sure you have everything ready before you leave. Again, this is simple, but it's there to use how you wish and to re-use based on the learnings from this holiday.

1) Create a new page, called "Packing list" and add it into this page.

2) Then try and replicate the below image, this is very similar to what we build in Chapter 2. Note, I did borrow some of this from the Notion free template. The packing list is of course not a full list.

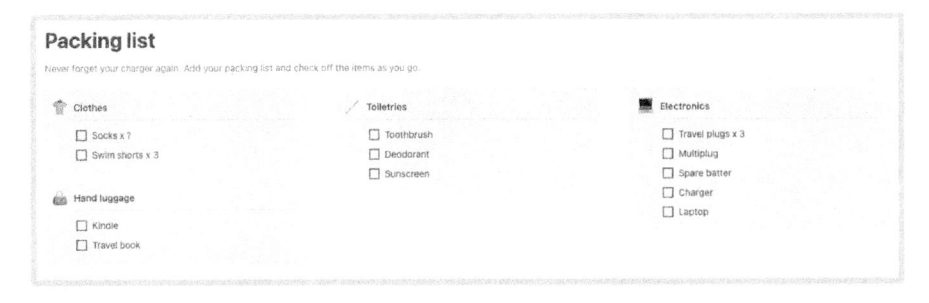

Packing list

Never forget your charger again. Add your packing list and check off the items as you go.

👕 Clothes
- ☐ Socks x 7
- ☐ Swim shorts x 3

🎒 Hand luggage
- ☐ Kindle
- ☐ Travel book

🪥 Toiletries
- ☐ Toothbrush
- ☐ Deodorant
- ☐ Sunscreen

🔌 Electronics
- ☐ Travel plugs x 3
- ☐ Multiplug
- ☐ Spare batter
- ☐ Charger
- ☐ Laptop

49

4: Travel Planner

3) Go back to "*Getting ready to go*" page and move the "*Packing list*" page to the right of the menu.

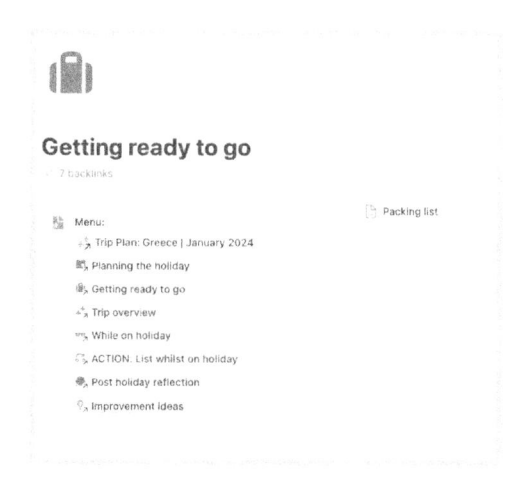

Getting ready to go
7 backlinks

Menu:
Trip Plan: Greece | January 2024
Planning the holiday
Getting ready to go
Trip overview
While on holiday
ACTION. List whilst on holiday
Post holiday reflection
Improvement ideas

Packing list

As a suggestion, you could add a "must buy list" to make sure that you get, for example factor 50 sunscreen. Or you could create standard lists depending on the type of trips you are going on, e.g. a ski list or scuba trip list.

Done. Isn't setting up Notion so simple now that you have learnt and applied the techniques. For the next page, we will strengthen our use of callouts to make better looking pages.

Trip overview setup

The purpose for this page is to have the key details you need to refer to whilst on the way, during and on the way back from the trip. This page focuses on flights, but you can add hotels, hire car details, or train times. Everything I have just mentioned is added on the next page, "While on holiday", but how you want this to work is up to you.

To create this page, we are going to make it look good with multiple callouts.

1) Recreate the below image, using 4 *callouts* - each use the same techniques you learnt whilst making the menu earlier. You will note two pages are embedded in the take-off details; we will come to their contents in the next step.

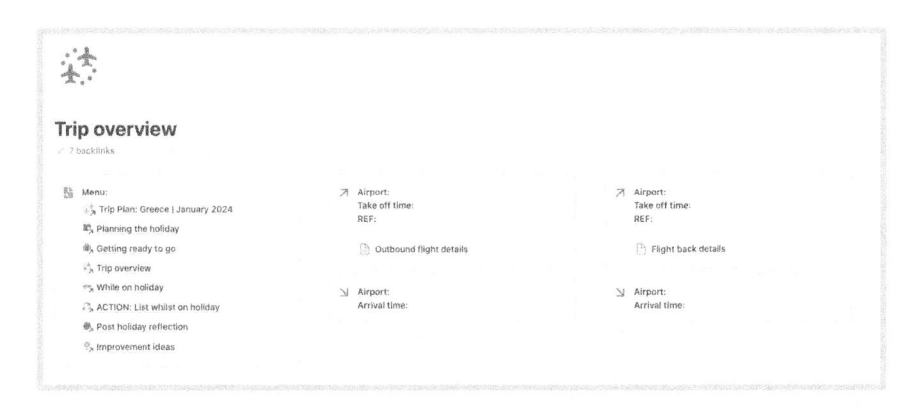

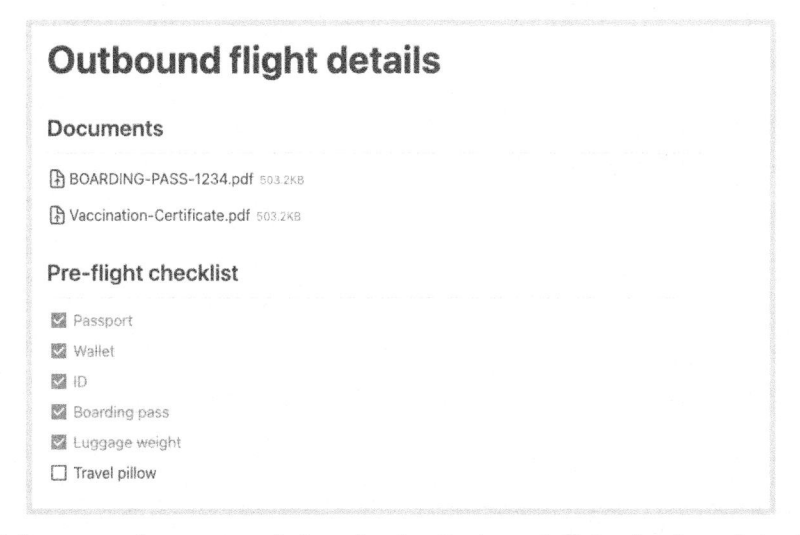

> **Trip overview**
> ✓ 7 backlinks
>
> 📖 Menu:
>   🍽 Trip Plan: Greece | January 2024
>   📝 Planning the holiday
>   🎒 Getting ready to go
>   ✈ Trip overview
>   🏖 While on holiday
>   ✅ ACTION: List whilst on holiday
>   🌴 Post holiday reflection
>   💡 Improvement ideas
>
> ↗ Airport:
>   Take off time:
>   REF:
>
>   📄 Outbound flight details
>
> ↘ Airport:
>   Arrival time:
>
> ↗ Airport:
>   Take off time:
>   REF:
>
>   📄 Flight back details
>
> ↘ Airport:
>   Arrival time:

> # Outbound flight details
>
> ## Documents
>
> 📄 BOARDING-PASS-1234.pdf 503.2KB
>
> 📄 Vaccination-Certificate.pdf 503.2KB
>
> ## Pre-flight checklist
>
> ☑ Passport
> ☑ Wallet
> ☑ ID
> ☑ Boarding pass
> ☑ Luggage weight
> ☐ Travel pillow

2) Re-create the contents below for the Outbound flight details and the flight back details. Again, this is one I borrowed from the Notion free template. Note you can embed the actual travel documents if you wish. I have done this as an example. You don't need to add them now.

This page was a little fiddlier, the next page uses even more techniques.

4: Travel Planner

While on holiday setup

The intent of this page is to be used day-by-day whilst on holiday. Like the other pages you will want to make this your own. For the one we will create here you will have the following:

- Google map of the place you are at
- Itinerary, with expense tracking and order of what's happening on that day in a Kanban board that you can move around.
- A journal and exercise tracker
- Personal rules to remember.

Let's start building it.

1) Add a Google map of the area we are going to. In your browser open Google maps and find where you are going to. Copy the URL/web address.

2) In the "While on holiday" page add "/google maps", it will ask for a URL and paste the one you have.

3) Move it to the right of the menu and resize it to what you want. See the image after step 7. This map has all the features you would get as if you were on Google maps. Really useful when you want to quickly check where something is. Remember though it will only work if you are offline, for offline maps you will have to use Google Maps directly.

4) Now we will build the Itinerary. For this we will create a database and use it in the board view. Let's create the database and set it up in table view. To do so set up and configure a database with four columns:

4.1) "Activity", type text.

4.2) "Day", type single select.

4.3) "Date", type date.

4.4) "Price", type number. Click the number format (see image below) and select your local currency. Note, you can also configure it to be the currency to mate the place you are going.

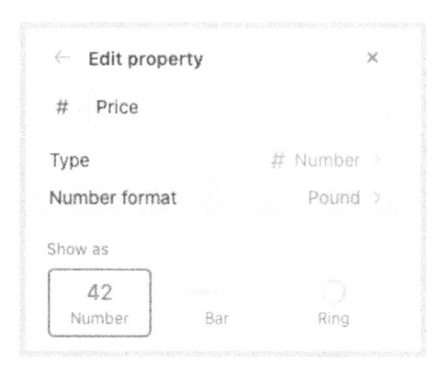

5) We will create some template pages to make the next view prettier and more usable. Create a page template for each of the following, for now the only difference will be the icons - you can see what I used in the image below.

    5.1) Arrive

    5.2) Leave

    5.3) Restaurant

    5.4) Taxi

    5.5) Sightsee

    5.6) Car hire

4: Travel Planner

You will see how this helps once we create the board view. You can edit the templates later to have specific things you want to remember, for example you can have the booking reference in car hire.

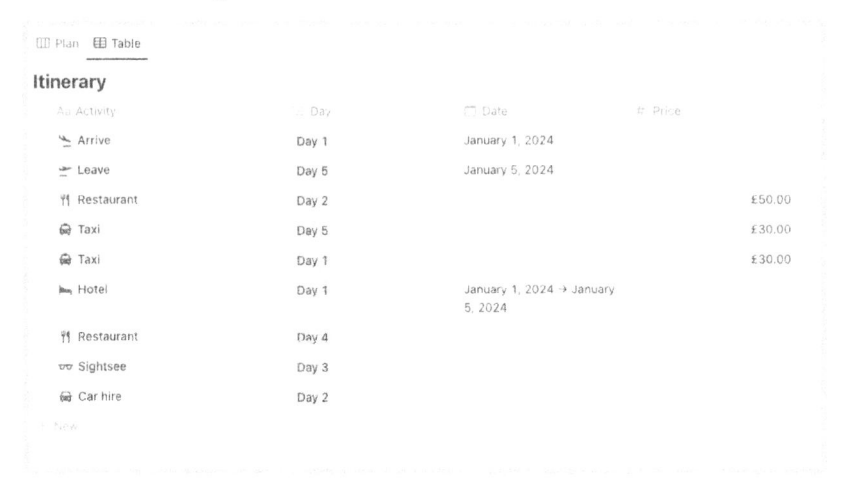

Activity	Day	Date	Price
Arrive	Day 1	January 1, 2024	
Leave	Day 5	January 5, 2024	
Restaurant	Day 2		£50.00
Taxi	Day 5		£30.00
Taxi	Day 1		£30.00
Hotel	Day 1	January 1, 2024 → January 5, 2024	
Restaurant	Day 4		
Sightsee	Day 3		
Car hire	Day 2		

6) Populate the database with the example data from the above image.

That's the database set up, now we will create the board view that we will use whilst on holiday.

7) Create a *board* view. Order by "Day" and make sure the Date is visible. Note the total next to Day in the image below - this is the total estimated spend per day.

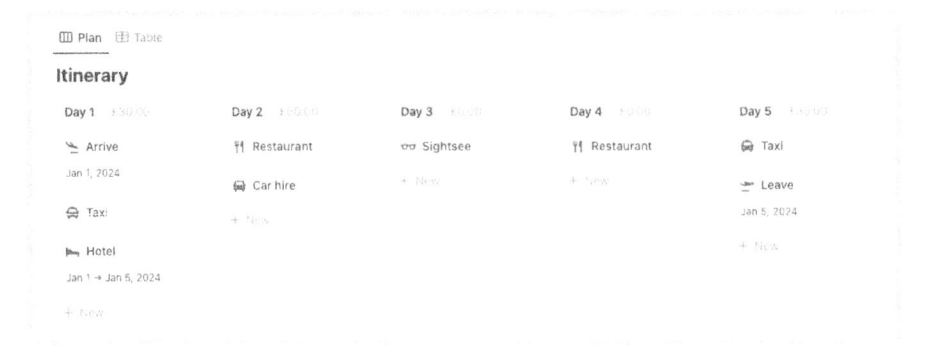

Itinerary

Day 1	Day 2	Day 3	Day 4	Day 5
Arrive	Restaurant	Sightsee	Restaurant	Taxi
Jan 1, 2024	Car hire			Leave
Taxi				Jan 5, 2024
Hotel				
Jan 1 → Jan 5, 2024				

Your page should look like the image below so far.

54

While on holiday

✓ 7 backlinks

Map

Menu:
- Trip Plan: Greece | January 2024
- Planning the holiday
- Getting ready to go
- Trip overview
- While on holiday
- ACTION: List whilst on holiday
- Post holiday reflection
- Improvement ideas

Plan | Table

Itinerary

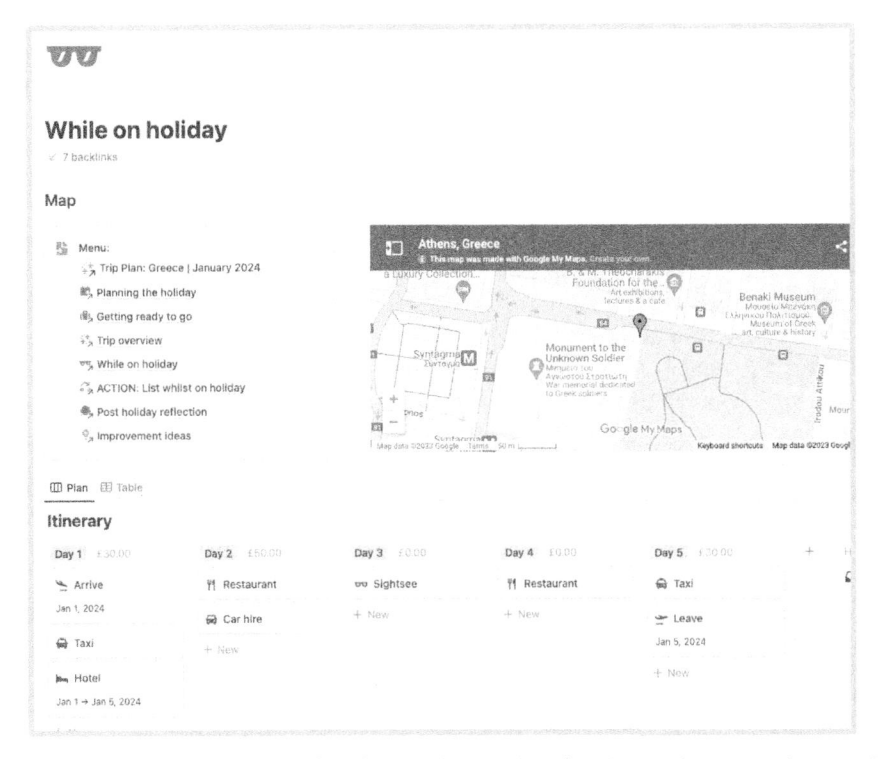

Day 1 £30.00	Day 2 £50.00	Day 3 £0.00	Day 4 £0.00	Day 5 £30.00
Arrive	Restaurant	Sightsee	Restaurant	Taxi
Jan 1, 2024	Car hire	+ New	+ New	Leave
Taxi	+ New			Jan 5, 2024
Hotel				+ New
Jan 1 → Jan 5, 2024				

Next, we will create a day-by-day tracker with rules. I use this to make sure I do the habits and to journal what you did each day. The above as a reminder is a plan, this new database is a capture of what happened. To create this, you will see a powerful way to use checkboxes.

1) Create a new *database* called "Day-by-Day" with the following columns:

    1.1) "Day", type text

    1.2) "Exercise", type text

    1.3) "Journal", type test

    1.4) "1 min plank", type checkbox

    1.5) "2 min plank", type checkbox

    1.6) "120 press-ups", type checkbox

    1.7) "80 squat thrusts", type checkbox

    1.8) "15 x 3 Leg ups", type checkbox

4: Travel Planner

1.9) "Daily Exercise", type formula - "if(prop("1 min plank") == true and prop("2 min plank") == true and prop("120 press-ups") == true and prop("80 squat thrusts") == true and prop("15 x 3 Leg ups") == true, "Done", "You can do it")". This will say "Done" when you have completed all the checkbox exercises. After creating this, move the column to the left of the checkboxes.

2) Create a row for each day.

I have given this as an example to help you learn. You can configure this work how you want. You also don't have to check exercise, it can track habits or even just reading so many pages of a book. I used something like the below example at an all-inclusive to make sure I wasn't just drinking and eating. The Exercise column was for a big exercise. The journal is just to write about the day. I hope you find this or one you configure yourself useful.

Finally, under the "Day-to-day" database we will do the following.

3) Create a /*toggle list* called "RULES" in bold.

4) Within the *toggle list* add "2 beers to water" or whatever rules you want to give yourself on holiday. You could have for example, wake up 2 days to watch the sunrise or try to learn a local word a day. These are just reminders.

The below section of this page should now look something like the below image and this page is done.

Note: You could have key actions for the day as its own type on the board if you wanted.

Actions on holiday setup

This is the page to use if you want to get a few things done on holiday. Anything from personal admin, to work commitments. You don't have to use this, but I find it is rare you have nothing to do on holiday, even if it's "pay that bill". This is the place that I write those down or if I have an idea, I store it here for when I get back. You can create this page with all the techniques you have learnt, so please try, and re-create the image below.

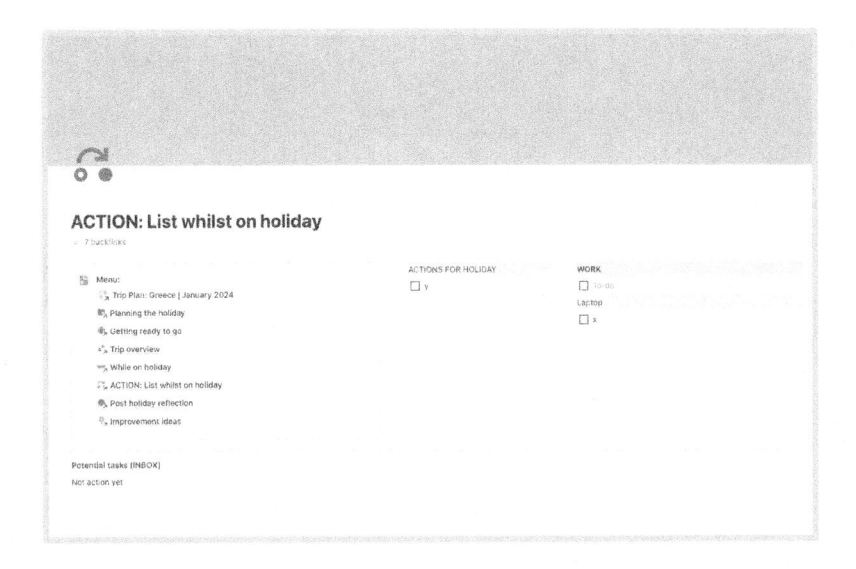

ACTION: List whilst on holiday

7 backlinks

Menu:
- Trip Plan: Greece | January 2024
- Planning the holiday
- Getting ready to go
- Trip overview
- While on holiday
- ACTION: List whilst on holiday
- Post holiday reflection
- Improvement ideas

ACTIONS FOR HOLIDAY
☐ y

WORK
☐ to-do
Laptop
☐ x

Potential tasks (INBOX)
Not action yet

Note the laptop section. I use this for things I need my computer for, so they are not things to do at the beach! I use the "Potential tasks (INBOX)" area to add things I may do or things I have come up with on holiday that I want to remember.

Another page done, well done.

Post-holiday reflection setup

The intent of this page is to reflect and write it down a week or two after your holiday. The questions are just ideas to get you thinking. The page is easy to create and is simple on purpose.

1) Recreate the image on the top of the next page.

57

4: Travel Planner

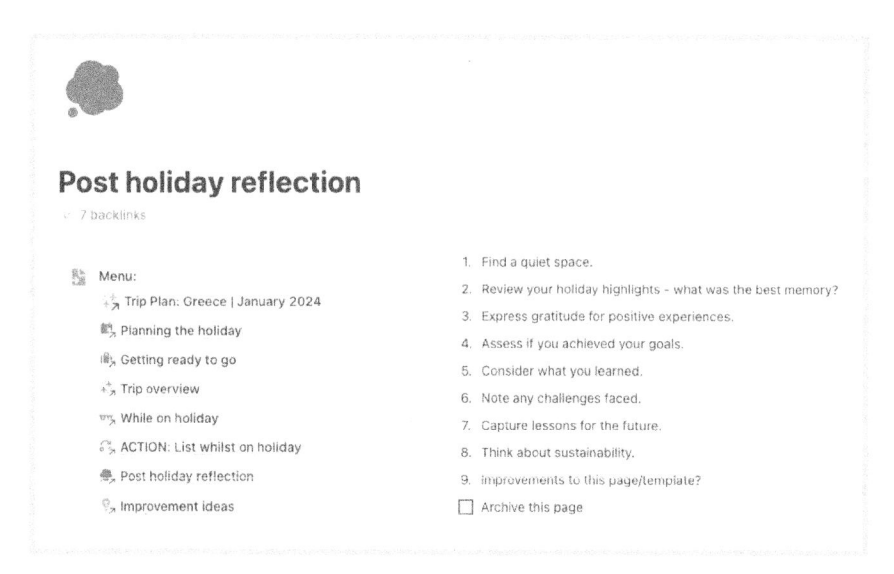

Post holiday reflection

7 backlinks

Menu:
- Trip Plan: Greece | January 2024
- Planning the holiday
- Getting ready to go
- Trip overview
- While on holiday
- ACTION: List whilst on holiday
- Post holiday reflection
- Improvement ideas

1. Find a quiet space.
2. Review your holiday highlights - what was the best memory?
3. Express gratitude for positive experiences.
4. Assess if you achieved your goals.
5. Consider what you learned.
6. Note any challenges faced.
7. Capture lessons for the future.
8. Think about sustainability.
9. improvements to this page/template?
☐ Archive this page

That's it for the set-up! We will leave the improvement ideas page blank. Please use this to think of your own ways of improving these sets of pages. When you do apply new ideas, you can even change the version number at the bottom of the home page as a mark of your developing success.

Making all of these into a repeatable duplicate

Now that we have a complete page, we want to re-use it, the simplest way is to create a duplicate. To do this

1) Click on the three-dot menu icon (···) at the top right corner of the latest trip page.

2) In the dropdown menu, select "Duplicate." A new duplicate page will be created with the same content as the original page.

3) Edit the duplicate page to remove any specific or sensitive information that you want to be included in the new trip, some specific areas:

3.1) The trip name and date

3.2) The cover image

3.3) The trip overview detail

3.4) Align the *"While on holiday"* page to match the direction of the trip. Easiest way to do this is in the taxble view to start with.

Summary

Hopefully you are now feeling all the previous skills you have gained have come together. I have purposely reduced the number of instructions in this chapter as I am confident you can start to create these multiple related blocks and pages from the idea itself in most cases. Also, I hope this trip planner helps you be more organized and get more from your valuable trips away.

Next, we will learn about linking databases together by building a full project and to-do list productivity system. Once you have completed that chapter; I have three challenges for you…

> **Challenge 1:** See if you can create a parent database for all your trips with status of the trip itself (planned, to be planned, been, etc.) that contains one of these trips for every row.

> **Challenge 2:** Link the to-dos in a trip to the to-do list you will create in the next chapter.

> **Challenge 3:** Make a trip a template in the trip database created in challenge 1.

Part 3: Personal task management system

Chapter 5 – Connecting databases with a Personal Productivity Management System

Build your own productivity/to-do system and tool by connecting Notion databases.

"The key is not to prioritize what's on your schedule, but to schedule your priorities."

Stephen Covey, author of "The 7 Habits of Highly Effective People"

> Areas covered in this chapter:
> - Connecting/linking databases together
> - Using synchronized blocks
> - Rollups
> - Automatic creation of data through templates

In this chapter we are going to create a productivity system. This will take Notion from a useful data capture/planning tool to the next level.

This chapter will focus on the databases and their set-up, ending with bringing them all together acting as an application. In the next chapter, we will use this foundation to create a full, end-to-end system with dashboards and views - making it much easier to use and understand the data within it.

Before we continue creating, we will spend some time touching on a few of productivity concepts. There is a lot of material online and in books about these systems, we will just cover enough to understand the foundation of how and why this productivity system was created the way it was.

Getting Things Done (GTD) System

GTD stands for "Getting Things Done," a productivity methodology created by David Allen. It is designed to help individuals manage tasks, reduce stress, and achieve greater clarity in their daily lives. The core principles of GTD include:

1. **Capture:** Collect all your tasks, ideas, and commitments into an external system. This could be a notebook, digital app, or any tool that works for you. This prevents tasks from cluttering your mind.

2. **Clarify:** Process the items you've captured. Decide whether each item is actionable or not. If it's actionable, determine what specific action needs to be taken and what the next steps are.

3. **Organize:** Categorize tasks and commitments into appropriate lists or categories, such as "Next Actions" (specific tasks to be done), "Projects" (larger undertakings with multiple steps), "Waiting For" (tasks that require input from others), and more.

4. **Reflect:** Regularly review your lists and categories to ensure that tasks are up-to-date, priorities are clear, and nothing is overlooked. This helps you stay on top of your commitments.

5. **Engage:** Choose tasks to work on based on context, time available, energy level, and priority. This ensures that you're working on the most important and relevant tasks at any given time.

The GTD methodology emphasizes the importance of keeping your mind free from constantly trying to remember tasks, deadlines, and commitments. By externalizing everything into a trusted system, you can focus more effectively on the task at hand, reduce stress, and make better decisions about what to work on next.

GTD has gained popularity as a practical approach to managing personal and professional tasks, and many tools and apps are available to help implement its principles. However, successful implementation requires consistent practice and adaptation to fit your unique needs and circumstances.

What is a Project (within a Productivity system)

In the context of productivity, a "project" refers to any multi-step, multi-action endeavor that requires more than one action to be completed. Projects can range from small tasks with just a few steps to complex, long-term undertakings. The concept of a project is important because it helps individuals break down large goals into actionable tasks, making them more manageable and achievable.

Key points about projects in productivity systems:
1. **Multiple Actions:** A project is not a single task; it's a collection of related tasks or actions that need to be completed to achieve a specific outcome or goal.
2. **Outcome-Oriented:** Projects have a clear outcome or result that you're aiming to achieve. The completion of all the associated actions will lead to this desired outcome.
3. **Concrete and Defined:** A project must have a clear definition and scope. It's important to identify what needs to be done, what the result should be, and what the steps are to get there.
4. **Diverse in Scale:** Projects can vary in scale and complexity. Some projects might involve just a handful of tasks, while others might require numerous actions spread out over weeks or months.
5. **Organizational Tool:** In the GTD methodology, projects are often captured and organized in a separate list or category called "Projects." Each project is listed along with its next action step to keep you focused on moving forward.
6. **Regular Review:** As with all GTD components, it's essential to regularly review your list of projects to ensure that they're still relevant, have the appropriate next actions assigned, and are aligned with your current priorities.

Breaking down goals and larger tasks into projects and individual actions helps prevent feeling overwhelmed and promotes a more systematic approach to productivity. By focusing on the next action required for each project, GTD encourages steady progress toward your desired outcomes.

The PARA System

The PARA system, developed by Tiago Forte, is a method for **organizing** information and tasks to enhance productivity. It stands for Projects, Areas, Resources, and Archives.

1. **Projects**: This category includes specific tasks and activities that you're actively working on. It helps you focus on your current goals and track progress.

2. **Areas**: Areas represent the different aspects of your life, such as work, health, hobbies, etc. Each area contains related projects and resources, aiding a holistic view of your responsibilities.

3. **Resources**: This encompasses reference materials, ideas, and information that you want to keep for future reference. Resources are organized within relevant areas for easy retrieval.

5: Connecting Databases & Productivity System

4. **Archives**: The archive holds completed projects, outdated information, and historical records. This prevents clutter in your active organizational space while retaining valuable information.

The PARA system enhances productivity by providing a structured framework to manage tasks, information, and goals. It reduces the mental load of juggling multiple responsibilities, makes it simpler to locate needed information, and ensures that completed tasks and information are appropriately stored. This system promotes efficient workflow, goal tracking, and overall organization.

Creating our "Thrive" Productivity System/Tool

When writing this book, I saw two main benefits for you, the reader. The first, was to learn Notion by doing and hopefully by now you are getting confident in your use of Notion and maybe even coming up with your own ideas and pages already. The second, was to give you a useful Productivity tool/system that you can use to replace a lot of those great applications out there as its configured just for you. This is where we will create that second goal.

With any great application or tool, it needs a cool name. Now you can just call it <your name> Productivity System or just Productivity System. For this example, I am going to call it the Thrive Productivity System. Why? As it sounds better, but also Thrive means to flourish and prosper, but not unnecessary/detrimental growth. We Thrive within our means; with the resources we have.

To start we need to create multiple databases, then link them. I will cover the latter once we have created two databases.

For Thrive, we will need four databases and you will see the link to the PARA system (although it's not a pure implementation of it, I will cover why when I get to the relevant sections) we covered earlier:

1. **Tasks:** Unsurprisingly this database will create all the data surrounding our tasks, whether they are individual, linked to a project, linked to an area or both the latter two.

2. **Projects:** This database will hold all our projects, whether they are stand alone or linked to an area.

3. **Areas:** This database will hold all the different areas of our life, work and personal items that we want to manage.

4. **Resources/Notes:** This data will hold all the different information pages/notes that relate to either an area, a project or again both. This is

a slight change to the PARA system. I have added Notes as a specific call out to reduce the amount of standalone text in a database item. You can still use these, but adding as an entity in itself allows it to be more easily shared.

This time we are going to create all our databases within a single page. This allows easier management of each of them and to edit them whilst comparing to others without jumping pages. You don't have to do this, but I find it easier for the "raw" databases. We will create lots of different views of this "raw" data throughout this chapter and in the next.

1) Our Productivity Tool will be within its own master page, so create a page called "Thrive - Productivity Management System". Feel free to name this how you like. I went with the normal settings of small text, full width and gave it the following icon.

2) Create our database page called "Thrive Databases", usual settings. You should have the below.

Initial Task Database Setup

Within Thrive Databases we will create our tasks database. As the name suggests this database will keep all the information associated with a task.

3) Create a new in-line database called "Thrive Tasks" in the Thrive Databases page.

4) Rename the table to "RAW Table". This will be the table view that shows all fields. Later, we will have views for specific reasons. Delete the 3 blank rows that were automatically generated.

5) Add the following columns to the database:

5.1) "Name", type text

5.2) "Done", type checkbox

5.3) "Due Date", type date

5.4) "DO Date", type date

5.5) "Context", type multi-select - these will be contexts from a GTD like system, e.g. @office or @call.

5.6) A emoticon flag - "▶", type checkbox

5.7) "Effort Est.", type number

5.8) "Effort Done", type number

5.9) "Created", type created time - this is the date the task is created and is automatically populated.

5.10) "Updated", type Last edited time - this is automatically populated each time the task is changed.

5.11) "Late", type formula, with the following formula - "now() > prop("Due Date") and formatDate(prop("Due Date"), "L") != formatDate(now(), "L")" This ticks a checkbox is the task is late from its due date, but not if it's late from the date you said you would do it (DO Date).

5.12) "Task Age", type formula, with the following formula - "dateBetween(now(), prop("Created"), "days")" This puts the number of days the task is old, as driven from the created date.

5.13) "Task Unchanged", type formula, with the following formula - "dateBetween(now(), prop("Updated"), "days")". This shows how many days it has been since you updated the task.

That's the database configured. You can even start populating it now with tasks if you wish.

Initial Project Database Setup

Now that we have a database that can hold tasks, we can create a database that can hold our projects.

6) In our Thrive Databases page, under Thrive Tasks Database add a divider line and then a new in-line database called "Thrive Projects".

7) Rename the table to "RAW Table". This will be the table view that shows all fields. Later on, we will have views for specific reasons. Delete the 3 blank rows that were automatically generated.

8) Add the following columns to the database:

8.1) "Name", type text

8.2) "Status", type status - the type status is very similar to the select type but allows you to filter differently and becomes pre-loaded with options. We will configure these in step 9.

8.3) "Goal", type text

8.4) "Last Review", type date

8.5) "Review Frequency", type select and add the following options:

- Weekly
- Fortnightly
- Monthly
- Bi-Monthly
- Quarterly

8.6) "Review Days", type formula, with the following formula - "if(prop("Review Frequency") == "Weekly", 7, if(prop("Review Frequency") == "Fortnightly", 14, if(prop("Review Frequency") == "Monthly", 30, if(prop("Review Frequency") == "Bi-Monthly", 60, if(prop("Review Frequency") == "Quarterly", 120, 0)))))". This is a lengthy one, but it is simple. It is setting a number of days based on the word you select in the Review Frequency column, e.g. Weekly = 7. This number will help us to calculate when the next review should be.

8.7) "Next Review", type formula, with the following formula - "dateAdd(prop("Last Review"), prop("Review Days"), "days")". This states the date the number of days after your last review. We use this to drive the GTD project review. Not all projects need to be reviewed weekly in my opinion.

8.8) "Overdue", type formula, with the following formula - "if(prop("Status") != "Done", now() > prop("Next Review") or empty(prop("Next Review")), if(prop("Status") != "Cancelled", now() > prop("Next Review") or empty(prop("Next Review")), false)). This will set a checkbox as ticked when a project is overdue for a review.

8.9) "Planned", type checkbox - this will be used to state if the project is planned or not, i.e. it has a set of tasks or it's just an idea with information.

8.10) "Created", type created time

8.11) "Updated", type Last edited time

8.12) Target Completion, type date

5: Connecting Databases & Productivity System

9) Let's go back and edit our "Status" options. A status type comes pre-loaded with options, these are within three categories - to-do, in progress and complete. We will set ours to match the below image.

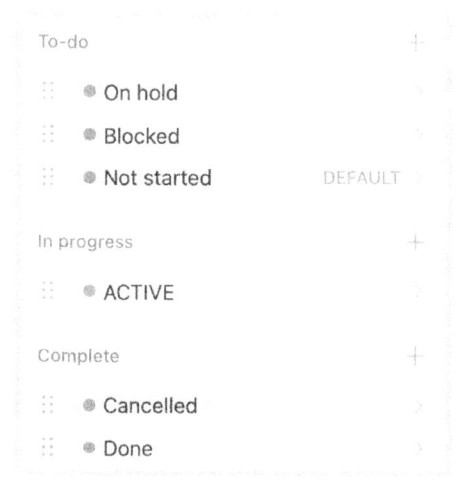

```
To-do                                        +
      ● On hold                              ›
      ● Blocked                              ›
      ● Not started           DEFAULT        ›

In progress                                  +
      ● ACTIVE                               ›

Complete                                     +
      ● Cancelled                            ›
      ● Done                                 ›
```

Note that "Not started" is set to default. This is one of the reasons we are using this type as it sets a default, where select doesn't. The other reason is the filtering, which we will use later, is much more user friendly.

We now have our second database created and are now able to capture our projects. In the next section we will link our projects and tasks databases so that we can have associated tasks to a project.

Connecting our Task and Project Database

Next, we are going to learn about arguably Notions most powerful feature - connecting different databases together. We will connect our Projects database to our Tasks database so that we can assign Projects to our tasks and see which tasks are associated with a single project. After this section we will create and connect other databases to this same area for Areas and Notes/Resources completing our PARA system.

Linked/connected databases are a way to connect different databases within Notion. It means that you can create a database in one page or workspace, and then link to it from another page or workspace. This can be incredibly powerful if you're organizing a large amount of information across different areas of your life or work. As we have discussed earlier this essentially makes our "applications" even more powerful.

10) In Thrive Projects, add a new column of type *Relation*, see below.

↗ Relation

11) Choose "Thrive Tasks" and select "Show on Thrive Tasks" - this creates a two-way relation, i.e. you can select a Thrive Project from a Thrive Task or vice versa.

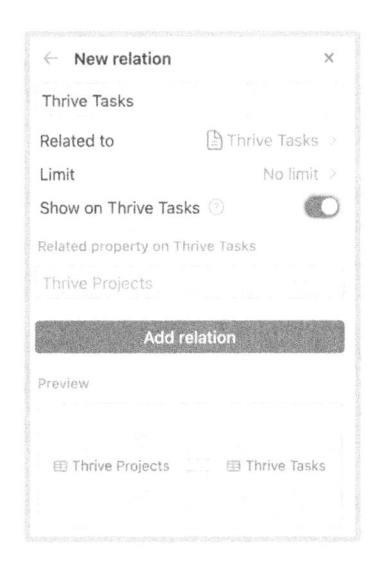

```
← New relation                    ×
Thrive Tasks
Related to              Thrive Tasks  >
Limit                       No limit  >
Show on Thrive Tasks              ⬤
Related property on Thrive Tasks
Thrive Projects

            Add relation

Preview

    ⊞ Thrive Projects    ⊞ Thrive Tasks
```

Let's spend a minute trying this out. Create a project in Thrive Projects, called "Thrive Project" and create three tasks in Thrive Tasks, called "Thrive task 1", "Thrive task 2" and "Thrive task 3".

In "Thrive task 1" go to the column that has been automatically created called "Thrive Projects" (see image below) Click it and you will see our new project called "Thrive Project". Select it.

Now, "Thrive task 1" is connected, and therefore a task of "Thrive Project". Hopefully you can now see the power of connecting these together. If you go to "Thrive Project" you will see the task, there too. This relation allows us to do reports and dashboards later, in the next few steps we will create columns to provide some of that date.

5: Connecting Databases & Productivity System

12) In "Thrive Projects" create some more columns, as below:

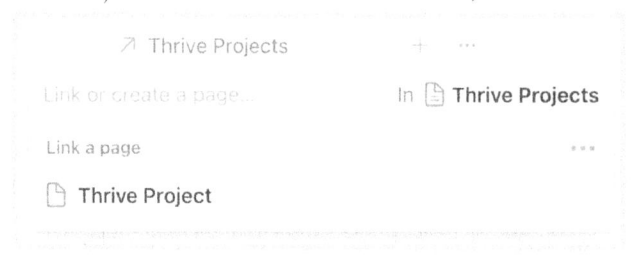

```
↗ Thrive Projects                    +   ...

Link or create a page...         In  📄 Thrive Projects

Link a page                                        ...

📄 Thrive Project
```

12.1) "# Tasks", type Rollup. Select "Thrive Tasks" and calculate based on "Count unique values" - see the image below. A rollup allows mini calculations to be done on a set of data within a database. In this case its counting unique tasks that would be associated with this project. In our case now that should be 1. This will dynamically change as we add or delete tasks. Note: it can't tell the difference between done and not complete tasks. In the next steps we can show that.

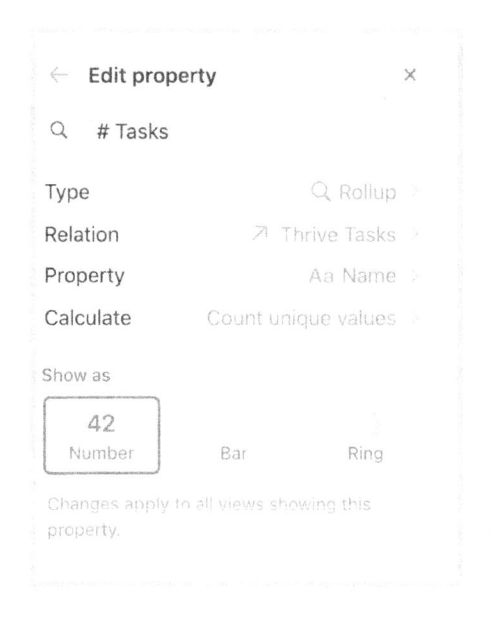

```
← Edit property                      ×

🔍 # Tasks

Type                          🔍 Rollup  >
Relation                   ↗ Thrive Tasks >
Property                       Aa Name   >
Calculate             Count unique values >

Show as

 ┌─────────┐
 │   42    │
 │ Number  │      Bar         Ring
 └─────────┘

Changes apply to all views showing this
property.
```

12.2) "Completed Tasks", type Rollup. Select "Thrive Tasks" and select Property "Done" and Calculate as "Checked" - see the image below.

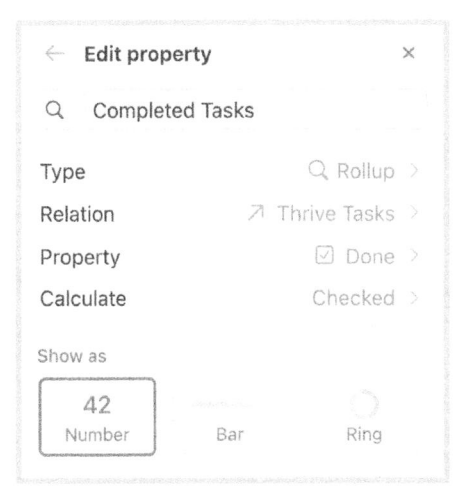

← Edit property ×

🔍 Completed Tasks

Type	🔍 Rollup >
Relation	↗ Thrive Tasks >
Property	☑ Done >
Calculate	Checked >

Show as

42		
Number	Bar	Ring

12.3) "Incomplete Tasks", type Rollup. Select "Thrive Tasks" and select Property "Done" and Calculate as "Unchecked".

12.4) "% Complete", type formula with the formula "round(prop("Completed Tasks") / prop("# Tasks") * 100)" - this will work out the % complete. Make sure you select Show as Ring as per the image below. We have introduced the "round" function this time, it just ensures we have a whole number returned.

71

5: Connecting Databases & Productivity System

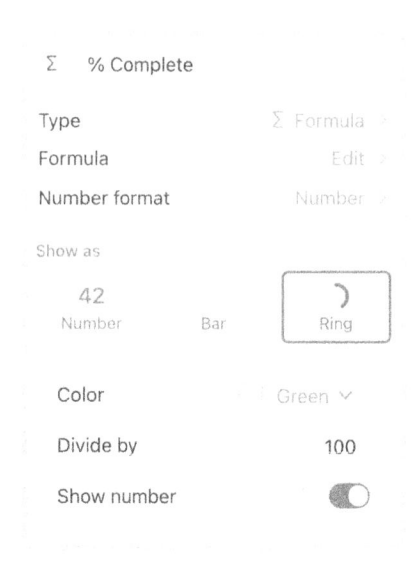

12.5) "Number of Tasks" type formula, with the formula "if(prop("# Tasks") == 1, ("✅ " + format(prop("# Tasks"))) + " task", ("✅ " + format(prop("# Tasks"))) + " tasks")" - Note the ticks are emojis. This will be used in dashboards later.

Let's create the other databases, connect them to our PARA system and add new fields to the existing databases where needed.

Create our Area Database

Now we will create our Areas database. As a reminder, an area is a consistent part of your life, whether it is work or personal that doesn't have an end (unlike a project). An area is likely to contain its own projects, tasks, and notes/resources.

13) In our Thrive Databases page, under Thrive Tasks Database add a divider line and then a new in-line database called "Thrive Areas".

14) Rename the table to "RAW Table". This will be the table view that shows all fields. Later we will have views for specific reasons. Delete the 3 blank rows that were automatically generated.

15) Add the following columns to the database:

15.1) "Name", type text

15.2) "Work/Personal", type select and add the following options:

- Work

- Personal

15.3) "Archive" type checkbox.

15.4) Add a relation to "Thrive Tasks", same as step 11)

15.5) "# Tasks", type Rollup. same as step 12.1)

15.6) "Number of Tasks", same as step 12.5)

15.7) Add a relation to "Thrive Projects", same as step 11)

15.8) "# Projects", type Rollup. same as step 15.6), only with it pointing to Thrive Projects

15.9) "Number of Projects", same as step 15.7), only with it pointing to Thrive Projects

15.10) "Last Review", type date

15.11) "Review Frequency", type select and add the following options:

- Weekly
- Fortnightly
- Monthly
- Bi-Monthly
- Quarterly

15.12) "Review Days", type formula, with the same formula as step 8.6)

15.13) "Next Review", type formula, with the same formula as step 8.7)

15.14) "Overdue", type formula - "if (now() > prop("Next Review"), true, false)"

15.15) "Updated", type Last edited time

As areas are persistent areas of. your life (unless archived) we have not included fields based on status or end goals.

That's our Area database, connected to our Projects and Tasks. The relations we have added here have automatically been added to those Thrive databases. We will make some additions to Thrive Areas after we create our Resources/Notes Database next.

Create our Resources/Notes Database

Finally, we will create our Resources/Notes database. As a reminder, resources/notes are data items that are related to a task, area or project that need documenting. They can be maintained, but they are not actions.

16) In our Thrive Databases page, under Thrive Projects Database add a divider line and then a new in-line database called "Thrive Resources/Notes". Delete the 3 blank rows that were automatically generated.

17) Rename the table to "RAW Table".

18) Add the following columns to the database:

18.1) "Name", type text

18.2) "Archive" type checkbox.

And that's it!

Now back to our Thrive Areas database, add the following columns:

19) Add a relation to "Thrive Resources/Notes", same as step 11)

20) "# Notes/Resources", type Rollup. same as step 15.6), only with it pointing to Thrive Areas

21) "Number of Notes/Resources", same as step 15.7), only with this function - "if(prop("# Notes/Resources") == 1, (" ✏ " + format(prop("# Notes/Resources"))) + " note", (" ✏ " + format(prop("# Notes/Resources"))) + " notes")"

We still need to add a few columns to our Thrive Projects database, go to this and add the following columns:

22) Add a relation to "Thrive Resources/Notes", same as step 11)

23) "# Notes/Resources", type Rollup. same as step 15.6), only with it pointing to Thrive Notes/Resources and when equal to Thrive Projects.

24) "Number of Notes/Resources", same as 21)

For this PARA system I haven't linked resources/notes to tasks. Other than tasks are part of the project concept in PARA the main reason is that a task is more transitory, and a Notion task can hold lots of notes. I have assumed that if a longer-term resource or note is needed it usually fits better with a project or area.

An example, with template for an area with associated tasks, projects, and resources

Let's bring this all together. For this we will also create a new area template.

Creating Database Templates

25) Create a new template (remember to click the drop-down arrow near the new blue button and select "New Template") in Thrive Areas and title it "New Area". The form should look like this.

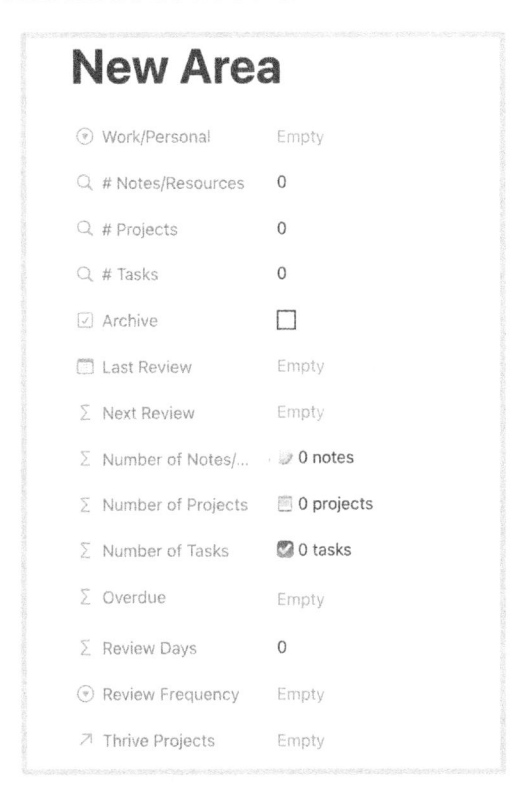

```
New Area

⊙ Work/Personal          Empty
Q # Notes/Resources      0
Q # Projects             0
Q # Tasks                0
☑ Archive                ☐
📅 Last Review           Empty
Σ Next Review            Empty
Σ Number of Notes/...    📄 0 notes
Σ Number of Projects     📰 0 projects
Σ Number of Tasks        ✅ 0 tasks
Σ Overdue                Empty
Σ Review Days            0
⊙ Review Frequency       Empty
↗ Thrive Projects        Empty
```

26) Hide all the fields that are not included in the image below step 27):

26.1) Hover to the right of the field and 6 dots will appear

26.2) Choose "Property visibility"

26.3) Select "Always hide"

27) After the first one, select hide at the bottom. Now as you hide other fields they will disappear. You can always view them again by clicking the rollup with x more properties before the main text are.

5: Connecting Databases & Productivity System

28) Now let's add some items to the body of the note that will be created each time we use this template. In the main body copy the below using header 2's. Note the dividers.

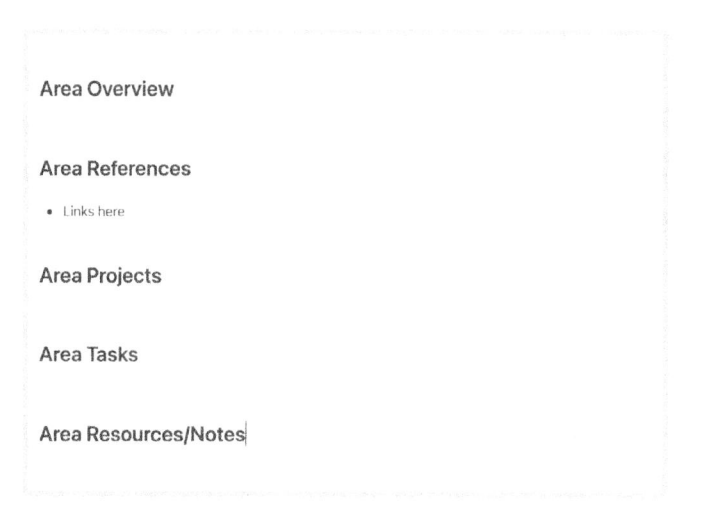

29) Now we will add an overview of the area, by using a Database view.

29.1) Add a *linked view of a database* pointing to *Thrive Areas*. Move this to in between the two dividers under "Area Overview".

29.2) Change the view to the below settings.

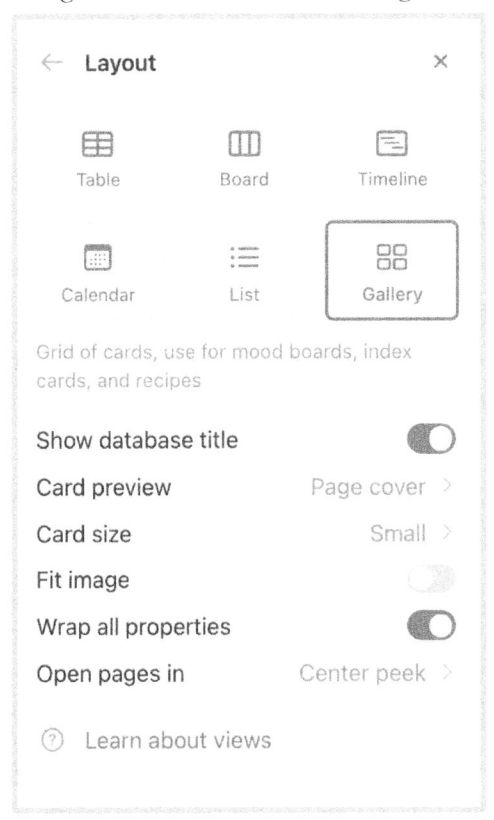

29.3) Display the following properties and note I have set to filter against name, but this is blank for now.

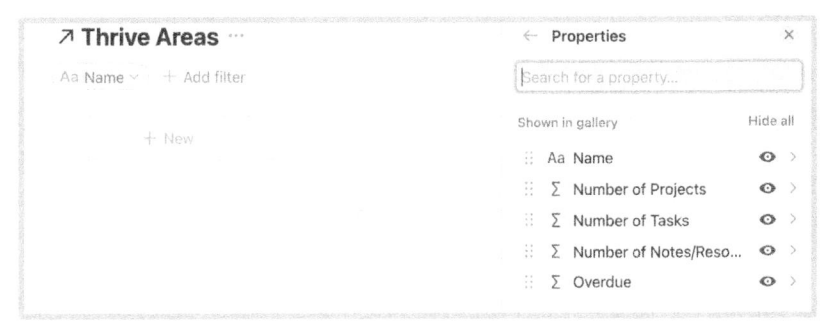

5: Connecting Databases & Productivity System

29.4) Next, let's add all projects that are related to this area. Add a linked view of the database pointing to Thrive Projects between the two dividers you created earlier under the "Area Projects" header. This time you can configure it as per above in the gallery or you can have a table or list. I will leave this to your choice. I use a table view personally. Make sure you filter on the "Thrive Area" equaling "New Area" (the title of this template). Then when you use this template, it will use whatever name you are giving for that area, therefore showing all projects that relate to this area.

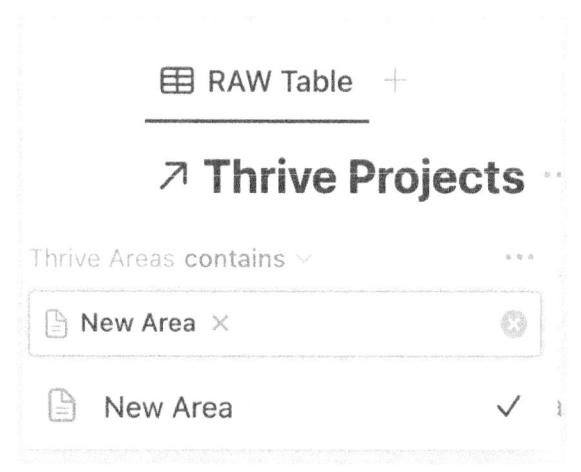

29.5) Repeat 29.4, only this time link to the "Thrive Tasks" database.

29.6) Repeat 29.4 and this time link "Thrive Resources/Notes" database

30) The template will automatically have been saved. Go to the Thrive Areas database and click the down arrow near "New". Next to the three dots on "New Area" select make default and do this for all Thrive Area views. Now when we click new it will automatically set to this template.

My Home Area example

Now that we have integrated all our databases and we have made a Thrive Area template it is easy to create a new area. Let's use an example that you can use.

31) Click the new blue button in "Thrive Areas" within the "Thrive Databases" page. This will automatically use the template we just created.

32) Title the page "Our Home" and set a nice icon and cover. I really recommend you upload a photo of your own house to make this look better within the dashboards we will create in the next chapter.

33) Set the last review date to today's date - manually

34) Make it Personal

35) Set it to whatever review frequency you want - I went for fortnightly, see image below.

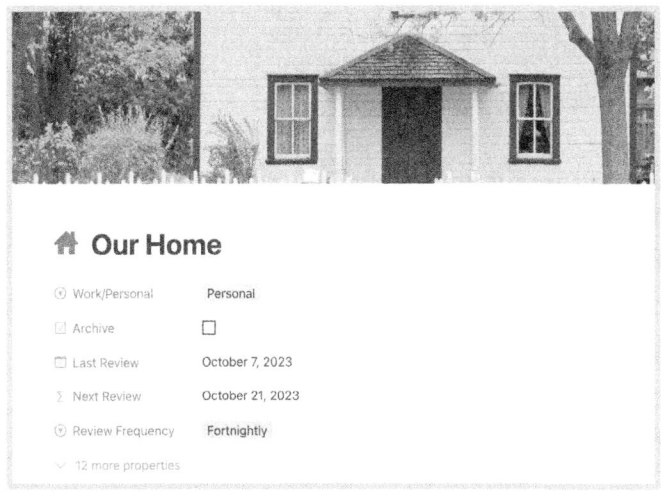

🏠 Our Home

Work/Personal	Personal
Archive	☐
Last Review	October 7, 2023
Next Review	October 21, 2023
Review Frequency	Fortnightly

12 more properties

35) Set filter in "Our Areas" to be name = "Our Home"

36) Now add house projects to projects, see challenge 4 at the end of the chapter on templates. Some examples:

- Redecorate the spare room
- Get solar
- Set up home WIFI mesh

  37) Add some home specific tasks, see Recurring tasks section later on home to make these recurring. Some examples:

- Fix the shower
- Clean out the fridge
- Buy a cabinet

  38) Add some resources/notes. Some examples

- Electric provider and tariffs
- What's in the loft
- Code for the shed lock

Hopefully this gives you a feel for the full system working.

79

Recurring tasks

A quick section on how we can create recurring tasks in Notion. This is a bit of a value-add bolt on to this chapter. We will use the Notion automation functionality to do this as at the time of writing this is the only way we can do it. I am sure Notion will develop functionality that will make this easier soon.

1) Create a task template within Thrive Project

2) Click the 3 dots

3) Choose when and how you want the task to repeat, remember if want weekdays change to weekly and select days

This is not a true recurring task for a full task management system - but it's close. The issue here is that you can't see the task coming before the date it is re-created.

Summary

Wow, you now have a fully working PARA productivity system. One that you can confidently configure to your needs. Now go create your projects and areas and in the next chapter, after we build some dashboards, you may even want to stop using your current app or system. At the very least, I hope I have shown the power of connecting databases. Next, we use the data from this system to present it better during the day, to plan for the week and view useful data and alerts by creating dashboards.

Challenge 1: Make a template for the Thrive Tasks database.

Challenge 2: Make a template for the Thrive Projects database, automatically show related tasks and resources/notes.

Chapter 6 – Bringing it all together with dashboards

Create dashboards to see what you need, when you need it in a well-presented format.

"Seeing is believing, but measuring is knowing."

Anonymous

> Areas covered in this chapter:
> - Insight databases
> - Functions within formulas
> - Dashboards

In the previous chapter we built the foundation of a productivity system. It creates and stores key data and even lets you link it. To add and view it you must use the tables. What we need is data and insights on the type of information we have. We need ways to bring key actions to our attention. For this and during this chapter we are going to build and use dashboards that use the databases we created in the previous chapter.

What is a dashboard

Firstly, Notion doesn't have a dashboard block or feature. When I refer to a dashboard I am referring to a concept. A dashboard is a highly customizable digital workspace that serves as a centralized hub for organizing and tracking our new PARA / GTD system. It shows key information that we need to act on and data that shows the general health of our system. All of this to be as visually pleasing as possible. Another way of looking at it is as your digital home page for data before you click into more detail.

6: Dashboards

In a way the template we created for an area in the previous chapter was a basic dashboard. Showing a report of how many associated tasks, projects and notes were associated with that area.

In this chapter we are going to build two dashboards:

- The **Today Dashboard:** A dashboard to make sure tasks that we need to do today are front of you. Remember today is the only day you can do a task. No matter how well you have planned a project, it does not get done until you take a small or big step forward today.
- The **GTD Dashboard:** A dashboard to view the overall health of our areas and projects, see where they need reviewing and to get key stats to help us manage our workload.

"Today" Dashboard

Arguably all that we have learnt and done throughout this book brought us to this point - the today dashboard. Remember, you only get things done in the now, everything else is just a planned activity, a dream, or an aspiration.

To build this dashboard we are going to bring together the different skills we learnt in previous chapters. We had a basic go of this in Chapter 2, but this dashboard will use the underlying data from the "Thrive" PARA system we created in Chapter 5. Let's build our first and as I said arguably most important dashboard.

Set the layout

1) Let's start with creating a new page within our Thrive - Product Management System called "Thrive TODAY"

2) Do the usual settings for full width and small text and add a logo and cover you like; I went with the ones in the image below.

Thrive TODAY

3) Add a call out to the top of the page, like the image below. This is where we will manually type our must do task, the one that if you achieve that one thing today you have moved something big forward. This is optional, and you could argue its repetition, you can after all your tasks driven from Thrive Tasks, but I find that having the manual box there forces you to think, review tasks and state which is the big one. By writing it down, you are committing to yourself.

> **Todays must:** This is my must do task

Tip: This task is usually the one you don't want to do, the one you have been holding back on. Force yourself to do it first or if you must schedule time to get it done. If you picked the right task, you would feel that you had a good day if even that was the only thing you got done. For more reading see the 1-3-5 task method or eat that frog.

Next, we are going to add insights. To do this we need to create a new database and make some changes to our existing databases.

Insights Database

4) Create new database in *Thrive Databases* called "Thrive Insights"

5) Configure it with the following columns:

5.1) "Name", type text

5.2) "Tasks", type relation, remember you name it when you set up the relation, see the image below. Note that it's called Insights in the *Thrive Tasks* database.

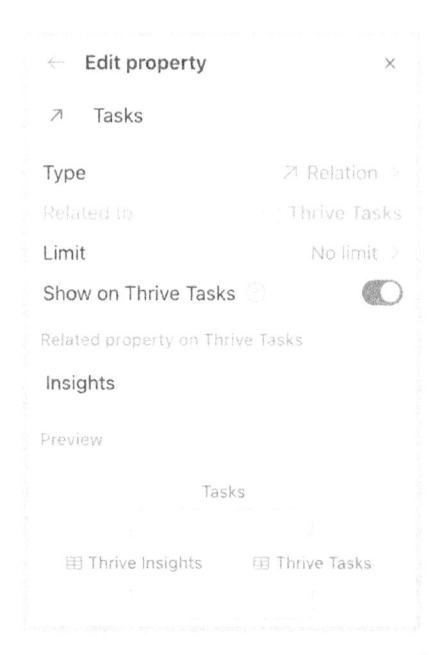

5.3) "# Tasks", type formula, with the formula "prop("Tasks").length()". This uses our first function where it outputs the length of the number of tasks in the database.

5.4) "# Late Tasks", type formula, with the formula "prop("Tasks").filter(current.prop("Late")).length()"

5.5) "Total Tasks", type formula, with the formula "Total tasks: " + format(prop("# Tasks"))". This is a more friendly way to display the data later.

5.6) "Late Tasks", type formula with the formula "Late tasks: " + format(prop("# Late Tasks"))

6) Delete the rows in the database.

7) Add a new row, with the name set to "Task insights". Later we will add a row for projects.

8) Go to Thrive Tasks and in the top row, select Task insights in the Insights column.

9) Then drag down, using the bottom right circle in the image below to set every row in Thrive Tasks to have Task insights in the Insights column.

> 📄 **Task Insights**

10) Next, we need to make sure that all new tasks in the future have this link in place, so go back to Thrive Tasks and create a new template, making sure you add "Task Insights" into the Task Insights column.

Let's take a moment to explain what we have just done. This approach isn't perfect, in a way we are getting around a Notion constraint by creating this insights database. By creating it, we can now start using the rollup feature below to count instances of various checkboxes that we have created, e.g. how many tasks are late. You will see the statistics are now working for the columns we created in steps 5.3 to 5.6.

Note that the total task number is the total of tasks whether done or not done.

Now that we have created our insights database with insights on our tasks let's go back to the Today view and add it.

11) Under the call out we added in step 3 add two columns.

12) In the left column:

12.1) Create a *linked view* of *Thrive Task Insights*. Use the gallery view, with card size small and no card preview. Add the "Total Tasks" and "Late Tasks" properties. It should look like the image below. Filter to Name = Task Insights. Then lock the view. Unfortunately, we can't remove the new option. As I said above, we are working with a constraint of Notion here to get what we need. I am sure they will add more powerful dashboard functions in the future.

▦ **Thrive Task Insights**

▼ Task Insights 1 +

Task Insights
Total tasks: 4
Late tasks:1

\+ New

12.2) Underneath the Thrive Task Insights gallery create a callout, with a red background, see below 12.3 as an example. This is our space to put quick actions that are not part of our Thrive system. This is here to quickly add and sort actions you need to do today. You should not lose attention from the Thrive actions in step 13.2. Also, don't let this get full or messy, see tip below.

> **Tip 1:** Throughout the day shuffle your next task to the top of the list, you can drag it.

> **Tip 2:** If you think of something that doesn't need doing today and could be done tomorrow or another day add it to Tomorrow.

> **Tip 3**: Save 10 minutes at the end of the day to tidy up Today and add tasks from it into your Thrive system. You may want to drag items from Tomorrow into Today so that you are ready the next day.

12.3) Then create a Tomorrow callout, with a yellow background.

> ▼ Today
>   ☐ Quick todo I just thought of
>   • Quick note
>   • Make sure I clean this up at the end of the day.
> ▼ Tomorrow

13) In the right column:

13.1) Create a call out like the below image. Remember to hold *shift* when pressing enter. We will add key links and pages within this box later.

> 🔗 **Key links:**
> Inbox
> Thrive Dashboard
> @Lists
> - Note you could have a specific project page here

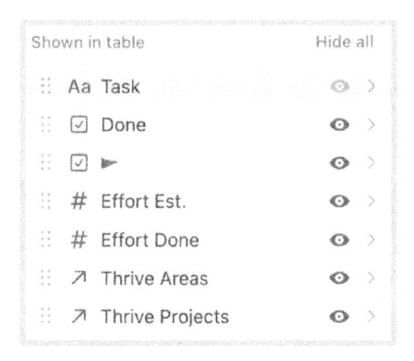

Shown in table	Hide all
Aa Task	👁 ›
☑ Done	👁 ›
☑ ▶	👁 ›
# Effort Est.	👁 ›
# Effort Done	👁 ›
↗ Thrive Areas	👁 ›
↗ Thrive Projects	👁 ›

13.2) Next, probably the most important part of the page. We will create three views of our "Thrive Task" database to show the work that we planned and therefore should do today.

13.2.1) Create the linked view of the Thrive Task database, underneath the call out we created in 13.1. Make it a table view, showing the below properties, in that order. Filter by "DO Date" and make it equal to *is before* and then select *Today*. Add a second filter by "Done" equals *unchecked*. Sort by flag, ascending.

It should look like the above image. Note we have the "Done" property next to "Task" so that you can click it when the task is done. It will then disappear from this view. You can of course add a new task into your Thrive system from any of these views.

13.2.2) *Right-click* on the table view name "DO Today" and select *Duplicate*. Call this new view "DUE Today". Add the property "DO Date", see image below. We are adding this as we want to spot where DO Date is not set to today in this case. This time create a filter by "DUE Date" and make it equal to *is before*

🔗 Key links:
Inbox
Thrive Dashboard
@Lists
- Note you could have a specific project page here

▦ **DO Today**

Aa Task	☑ Done	☑ ▶	# Effort Est.	# Ef

No filter results. Click to add a row.
+ New

and then select *Today*. Remove the "DO Today" filter.

87

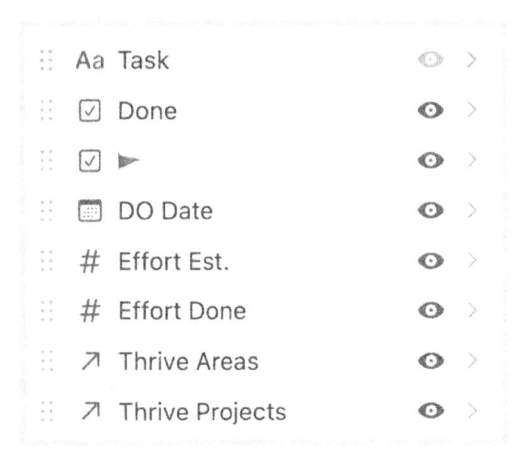

13.2.3) Create a view called "Late Tasks". This time you will have to select the three-dots after the view name. See the image below.

Set up with the below properties visible. Add a filter with "DO Date" with *is before* and select *Today*. Add a filter with "DUE Date" with *is before* and select *Today*. Sort by "DUE Date" *ascending*.

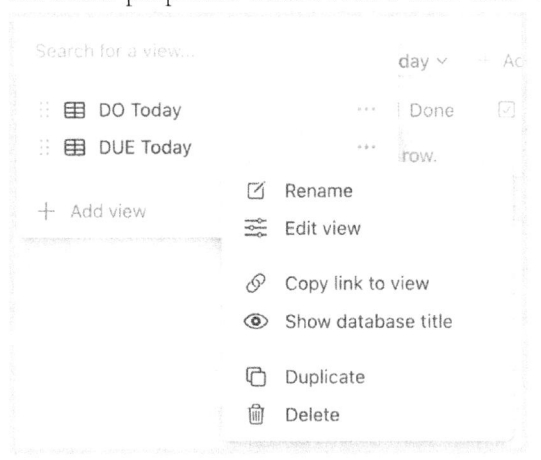

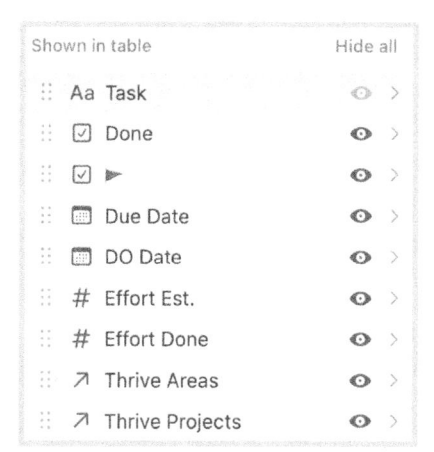

Shown in table	Hide all
Aa Task	👁 >
☑ Done	👁 >
☑ ▶	👁 >
📅 Due Date	👁 >
📅 DO Date	👁 >
# Effort Est.	👁 >
# Effort Done	👁 >
↗ Thrive Areas	👁 >
↗ Thrive Projects	👁 >

The idea of this view is that we can select alternate DUE and DO dates if we can't do it today or set it to today if we intend to do it today.

14) Add a divider below the two columns, like in the image below.

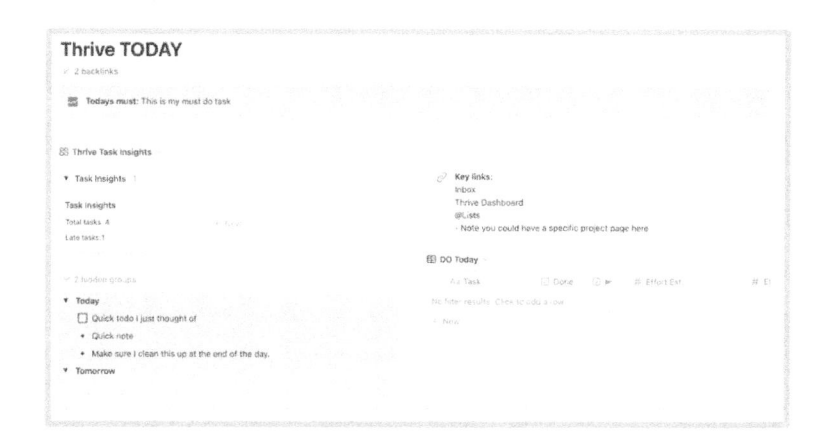

15). Next, we will create a scratch pad for quick notes, minutes, etc.

15.1) Add a h*eader 2* below the divider with a grey background. Call it "Scratch Pad"

15.2) Create a new in-line database, call it "Scratch Pad". Give it three properties:

Name, type text

Created, type Created

Updated, Last updated

6: Dashboards

15.3) Use the gallery view, with medium tile size. Card preview is set to *Card Content*. You can see how it looks with an example page/entry added below step 16).

16) Add a *divider* under the Scratch pad database

17) Add a *call out under the divider*. I use this space to add quotes that are making me think now. See the image below for an example.

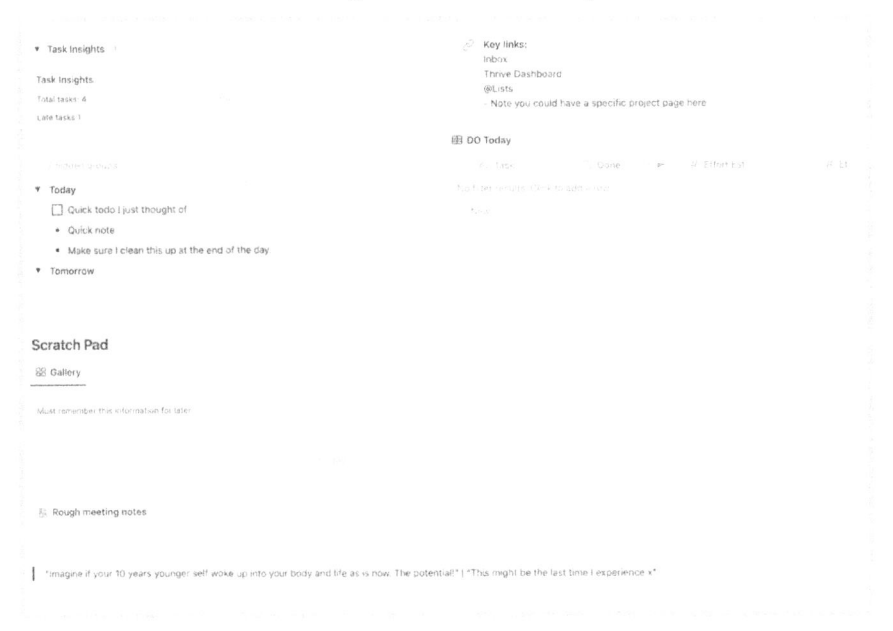

That's the main structure of the page, now let's go back and create the links we described in step 13.2.1.

18) For our inbox we can either add a link to the inbox page we created in Chapter 2 or create a new page. To make a clean example I am going to create a new page as this one will link to our Thrive Tasks. Highlight "Inbox" and

type /page and add a new page. I have done the usual set-up so that it looks like the below image.

Inbox
Empty page

Remember we described what the inbox is used for in Chapter two.

18.1) Create a Toggle List, with a light grey background and with a bold title "Quick Inbox:

18.2) Linked view of Thrive Tasks, hide the database title. Set-up with the following properties viable.

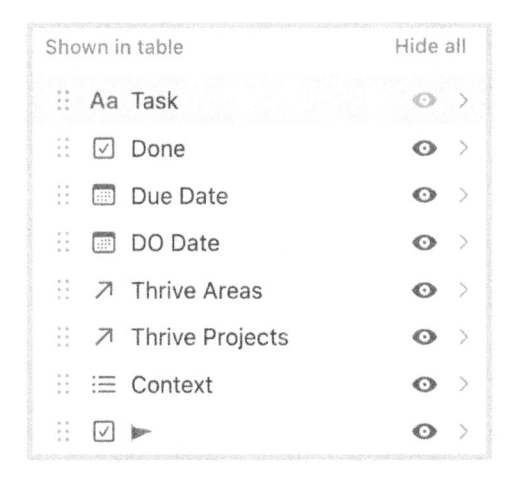

Shown in table	Hide all
Aa Task	👁 >
☑ Done	👁 >
📅 Due Date	👁 >
📅 DO Date	👁 >
↗ Thrive Areas	👁 >
↗ Thrive Projects	👁 >
≡ Context	👁 >
☑ ▶	👁 >

18.3) Filter where "Done" is *unchecked*, "Thrive Projects" is *empty* and "Thrive Areas is *empty*. We are doing this as we are trying to catch tasks that are not part of our organized system. In other words, they are not part of a project or area. This is a space where you can order them into those spaces. You can have a project for single tasks if you want.

91

6: Dashboards

Your inbox should like the image below.

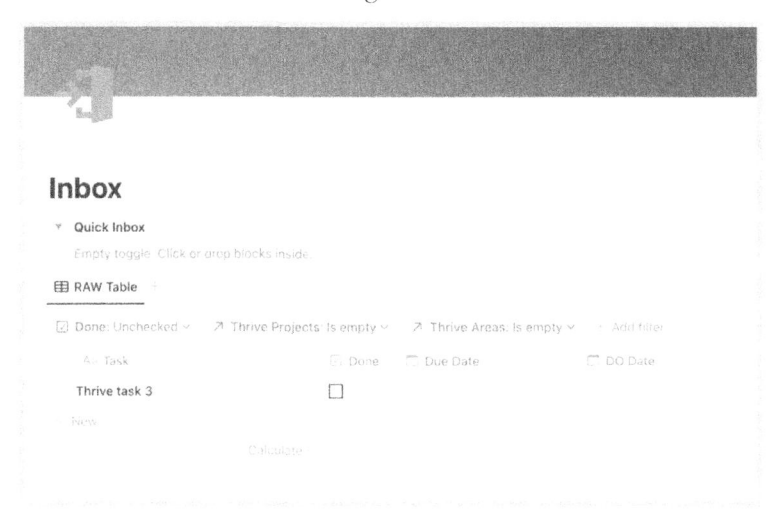

Inbox

▼ Quick Inbox
    Empty toggle. Click or drop blocks inside.
⊞ RAW Table
☑ Done: Unchecked ∨   ↗ Thrive Projects: Is empty ∨   ↗ Thrive Areas: Is empty ∨   + Add filter

Task	Done	Due Date	DO Date
Thrive task 3	☐		

+ New

Calculate

19) For our @lists highlight "@lists" and type /page and add a new page. I have done the usual set-up so that it looks like the below image.

@lists

Tip 4: An @ or "at" list is my naming of contexts in Getting Things Done (GTD). A context list is a list of tasks grouped together based on the context or situation in which they can be accomplished. Contexts are typically related to the tools, resources, or circumstances required to complete a task. Examples of common contexts include "@home," "@work," "@errands," "@phone," "@computer," etc. I personally add people to this list, either something you want to say to the person (either assigning a task or telling them something), or something you are waiting for them to do/tell you.

The purpose of context lists is to organize tasks based on where or how they can be done, making it easier for you to focus on tasks that are relevant and feasible given their current location or situation. This approach helps enhance productivity by allowing users to efficiently select and tackle tasks based on their context, rather than having to sift through a long list of tasks that may not be relevant now.

19.1) On this page I then create a sub-page for each context/@ list I care about. An example can be seen below with two examples @lists. One for tasks I want to do on the train and another for during my lunch.

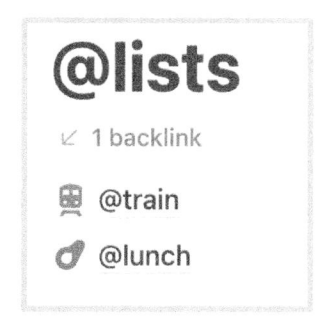

@lists

↙ 1 backlink

🚆 @train

🥑 @lunch

19.2) Within each sub-page I create a view of Thrive Tasks and filter on the context, see image below. I also have a quick entry toggle list, like 17.1 for our Inbox.

6: Dashboards

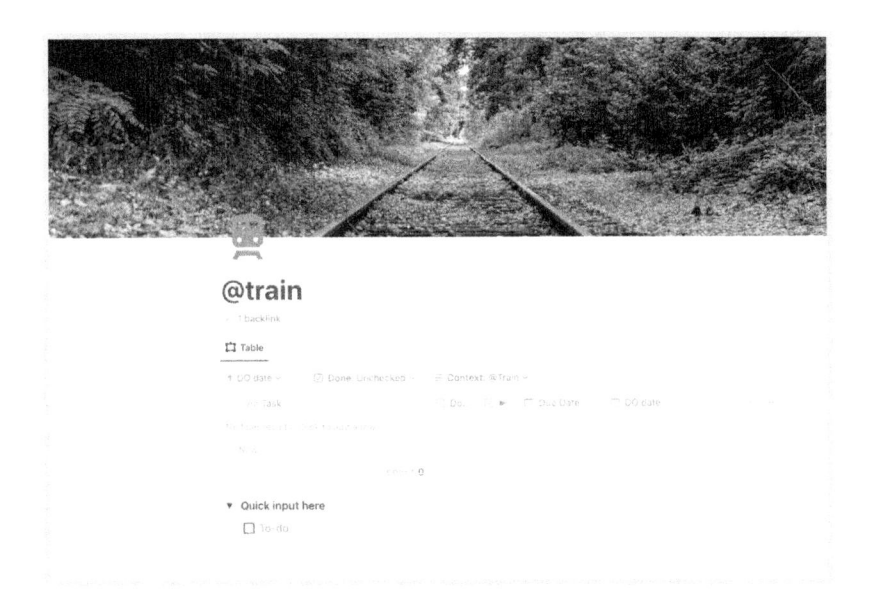

20) Finally, we will create a specific link for one of our Projects, we could do this for an area as well.

20.1) Go to Thrive Projects and open "Thrive Project", our example project. Click the three dots in the top right and select *Copy link*, see the image below.

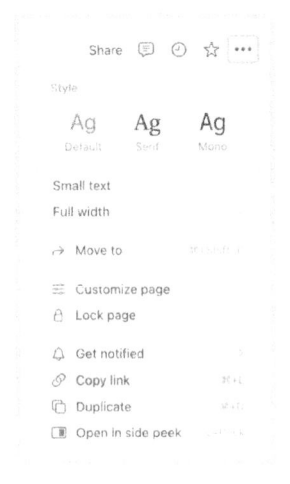

20.2) Where we had "- Note you could have a specific project page here" replace this with the link, remember to hit enter and it will create a short version. It should look like the image below.

> Key links:
> Inbox
> @lists
> Thrive Dashboard
> Thrive Project

20.3) (optional) I am not suggesting you have all your projects/areas in key links, but it can be useful to have some key ones. Remember you can *favorite* the project page by clicking the star and it will go to your left-hand menu.

We will come back to the links area and add a link to our Thrive Dashboard that we will create next. Your Today page should be something like the image on the next page.

If you like this new dashboard then don't forget to delete the Today and Inbox pages, we created in chapter 2.

95

6: Dashboards

> **Challenge 5:** Create a template within the scratch pad database (in Thrive TODAY) for formal meeting minutes. This is something that would be well placed in Resources / Notes of your PARA system.

Thrive Dashboard

Whilst all your actions are done (well seen) via the Today Dashboard we need to create a view of our Thrive system so that we can plan, track progress, and ensure the right tasks are seen at the right time. We will do this with the last dashboard we will create in this book - the Thrive Dashboard. Let's start our last project together.

1) Create a new *Page* in Thrive - Productivity Management System called "Thrive Dashboard". Usual settings and made mine look like the image below.

Thrive Dashboard
Empty page

2) Add a *Table of Contents* element and then create the following *h1* and *h2* headers. Give them different background colors and separate them with *divider* elements. It will look something like the image below.

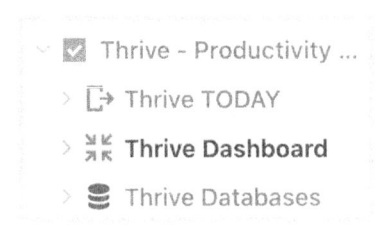

- Thrive - Productivity ...
  - Thrive TODAY
  - **Thrive Dashboard**
  - Thrive Databases

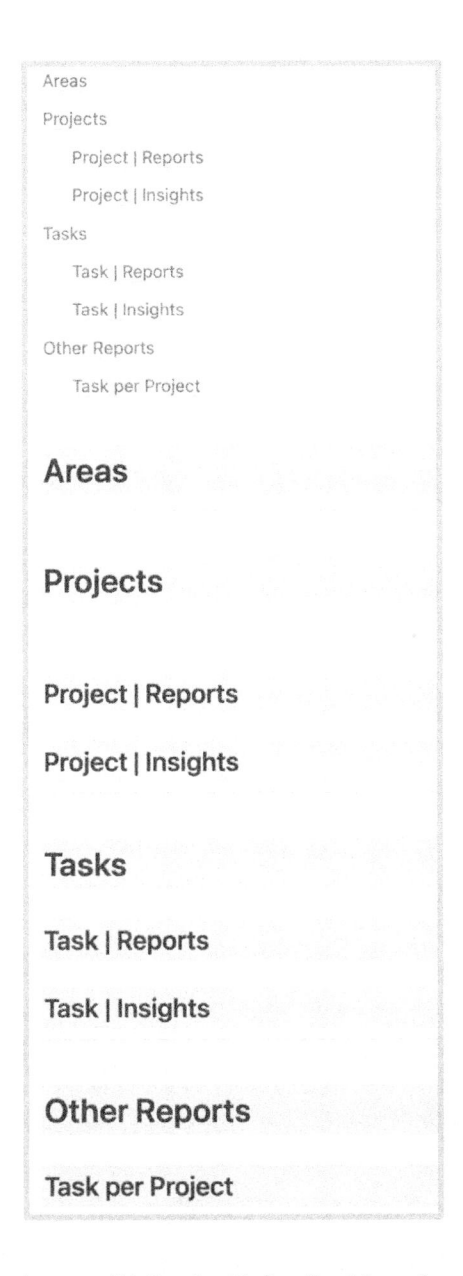

> Areas
> Projects
>   Project | Reports
>   Project | Insights
> Tasks
>   Task | Reports
>   Task | Insights
> Other Reports
>   Task per Project
>
> # Areas
>
> # Projects
>
> ## Project | Reports
>
> ## Project | Insights
>
> # Tasks
>
> ## Task | Reports
>
> ## Task | Insights
>
> # Other Reports
>
> ## Task per Project

3) Similar to what we did for the Today Dashboard, we will create a links box. We will put this to the side of our *Table of Contents*.

6: Dashboards

3.1) Create the links box by creating a *call out* element. Give it a white background and set it up so it looks like the below image with the links to the relevant pages and the same icon. See step 19 in the Today Dashboard in this chapter if you need to remember how to do this.

3.2) Type "/2 columns" and then drag the Table of Contents to the left side.

3.3) Drag the call out element with our links in it to the right of our Table of Contents. It should now look like the below image.

3.4) Go back to our Today Dashboard and replace the dummy link to our GTD Dashboard to a link to this new page.

4) Next, we will create our views of our Thrive Area database.

4.1) Under the *h1* entitled "Areas", but above the *divider*, add a *linked view of database* of the "Thrive Areas" database. Choose a gallery view with *card preview* set to *Page cover*. *Card size* Small. Hide the database title and name this view "My Areas". It should look something like the below image.

4.2) Now let's make the following properties visible:

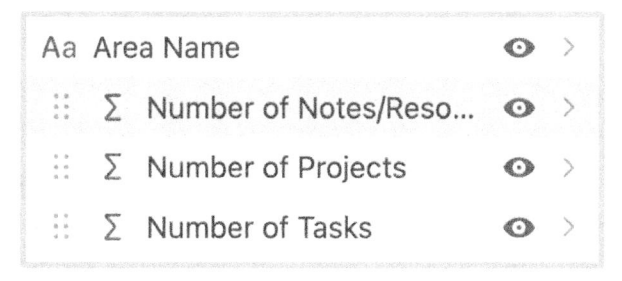

4.3) We will add a new property to our Thrive Areas database. Go back to this database and add another formula property called "Review Needed. The formula is "if(prop("Overdue") == true, "!! Review needed!", "")". This will display an alert when the area needs to be reviewed. Make this property visible too. Now our space should look like the image below.

Areas

⊞ My Areas +

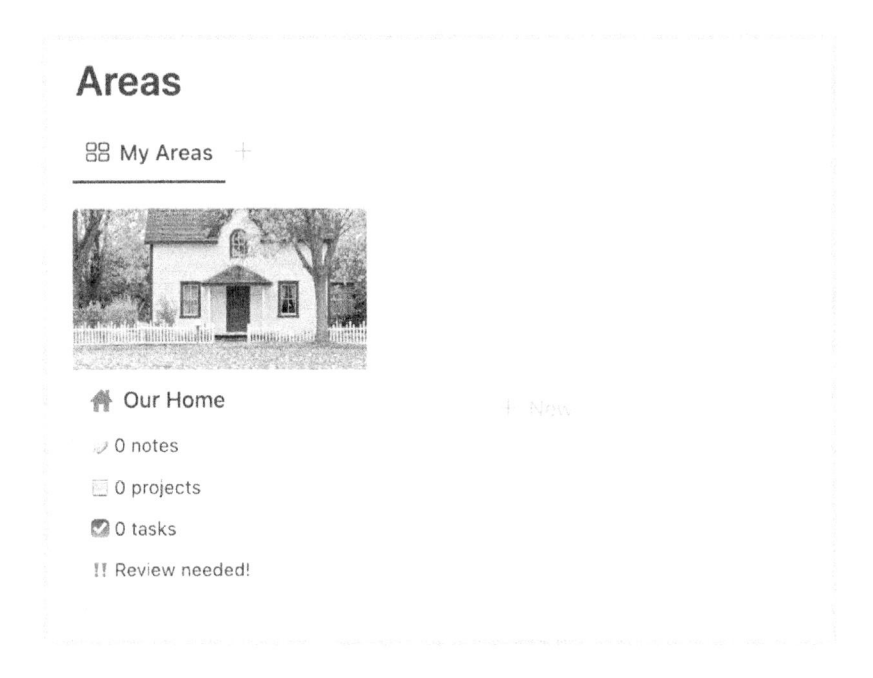

🏠 Our Home

◌ 0 notes
☐ 0 projects
☑ 0 tasks
‼ Review needed!

4.4) Even though we are flagging when areas need reviews, we can make it easier for ourselves by creating a view just for this. Duplicate the "My Areas" view, call it "Review Needed" and then add a filter of "Overdue" equals *checked*.

4.5) We will now create two more views to show all personal areas and all work areas. Repeat step 4.4, only this time call the first view "Personal Areas" and the second view "Work Areas". Have a filter "Personal/Work" set to either work or personal depending on the view.

You should now have something like the below image.

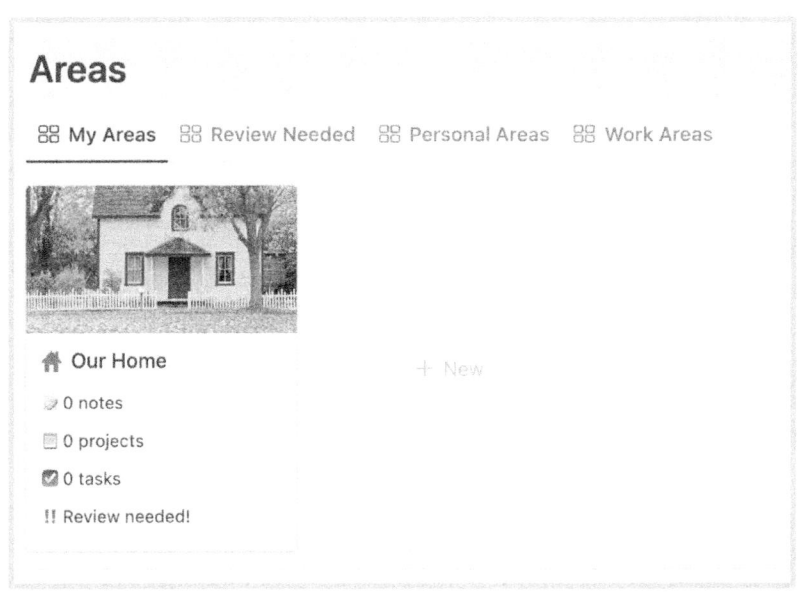

Having the multiple view may seem over the top now but will be particularly good as your areas grow. They will be even more powerful when applied to projects, which we are going to do next.

5) Next, we will create our views of our Thrive Projects database.

5.1) Under the *h2* entitled "Project | Reports", add a *linked view of database* of the "Thrive Projects" database. Choose a gallery view with *card preview* set to *Page cover*. *Card size* Small. Hide the database title and name this view "Active Projects". Filter by Status = "Active". If you still have the dummy projects that we created in Chapter 5 then go back to "Thrive Project" in "Thrive Projects" and set its status to "Active", this way you can at least test the view.

5.2) Now let's make the following properties visible:

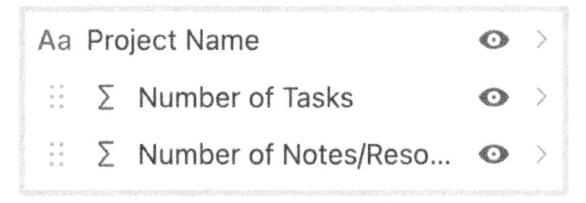

6: Dashboards

5.3) Like with Areas, we will add a new property to our Thrive Projects database. Go back to this database and add another formula property called "Review Needed. The formula is "if(prop("Overdue") == true, "!! Review needed!", "")". This will display an alert when the area needs to be reviewed. Make this property visible too. I edited the data within "Thrive Project" to make it need a review. With this the view should look like the image below.

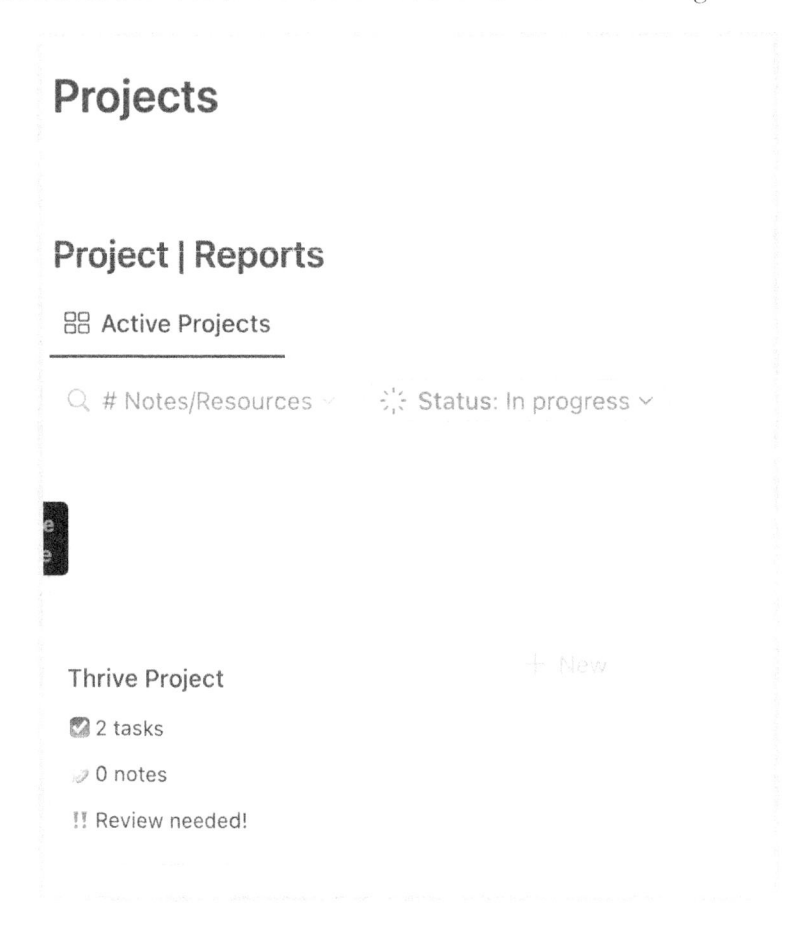

Projects

Project | Reports

⊞ Active Projects
───────────────

🔍 # Notes/Resources ⌄   ✦ Status: In progress ⌄

Thrive Project   + New

☑ 2 tasks

📎 0 notes

!! Review needed!

5.4) Like Areas above, we can make it easier to see Projects that needs a review by creating a view just for this. So, duplicate the "Active Projects" view, call it "Active: Review Needed" and then add a filter of "Overdue" equals *checked*.

5.5) Our next view will be Active (i.e. in progress projects) that need planning. This is done by duplicating the last view, call it "Active: No Plan". Remove the Overdue filter and add a filter for "Planned" equal to *unchecked*.

5.6) Our last two Thrive Projects views will show all personal areas and all work areas. Before doing this, we need to go back to our Thrive Projects database and add a Select type, called "Personal/Work", with two options "Work" and "Personal. Then go back to Thrive Dashboard and duplicate the last project view, call the first view "All Work Projects" and the second view "All Personal Projects". Remove all filters and then have a filter on "Personal/Work" set to either work or personal depending on the view.

Your dashboard should look like the image below.

6) Just like the Task Insights we added to our Today Dashboard we will do the same with Projects.

6.1) Go to *Thrive Databases* and in *Thrive Insights* and add a row. For *Name* type "Project Insights". We are going to add columns specifically to Projects as we can't use the task ones. We can make the task's stats invisible when we come to view the insights.

6.2) Add the following columns to *Thrive Insights:*

- "# Projects", type *Formula*, with the formula "prop("Projects").length()"
- "# Active Projects", type *Formula*, with the formula "prop("Projects").filter(current.prop("Status") == "ACTIVE").length()"
- Right click on *# Active Projects* and select *Duplicate property*. This means the already inserted formula from above is easy to edit. Name the property "#

On Hold Projects" Edit the *Formula to be* "prop("Projects").filter(current.prop("Status") == "On hold").length()"
- Duplicate again. Name the property "# Blocked Projects" Edit the *Formula to be* "prop("Projects").filter(current.prop("Status") == "Blocked").length()"
- Duplicate again. Name the property "# Not Started Projects" Edit the *Formula to be* "prop("Projects").filter(current.prop("Status") == "Not started").length()"
- Duplicate again. Name the property "# Cancelled Projects" Edit the *Formula to be* "prop("Projects").filter(current.prop("Status") == "Cancelled").length()"
- "Total Projects", type *Formula,* with the formula ""Total projects: " + format(prop("# Projects"))"
- Duplicate "Total Projects", called it "Total Active Projects", with the formula ""Total active projects: " + format(prop("# Active Projects"))"
- Duplicate again, called it "Total On Hold Projects", with the formula ""Total on-hold projects: " + format(prop("# On Hold Projects"))"
- Duplicate again, called it "Total Blocked Projects", with the formula ""Total blocked projects: " + format(prop("# Blocked Projects"))"
- Duplicate again, called it "Total Not Started Projects", with the formula ""Total not started projects: " + format(prop("# Not Started Projects"))"
- Duplicate again, called it "Cancelled Projects", with the formula ""Total cancelled projects: " + format(prop("# Cancelled Projects"))"

6.3) Go back to *Thrive Dashboard*, under the *Project Insights header*. Insert a *linked view of database* for "Thrive Insights". Choose the Gallery view, with large tiles. Hide the database name and filter "Name" = "Project". Make the following properties visible.

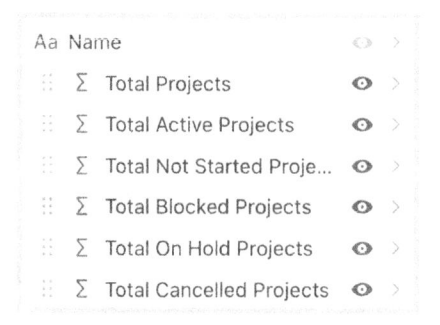

Aa Name	
Σ Total Projects	👁 >
Σ Total Active Projects	👁 >
Σ Total Not Started Proje…	👁 >
Σ Total Blocked Projects	👁 >
Σ Total On Hold Projects	👁 >
Σ Total Cancelled Projects	👁 >

The insights' view should look like the image below.

![Project | Insights gallery view showing Project Insights: Total projects: 2, Total active projects: 1, Total not started projects: 1, Total blocked projects: 0, Total on hold projects: 0, Total cancelled projects: 0]

7) Next, we will create our views of our Thrive Tasks database.

7.1) Under the *h2* entitled "Task | Reports", add a *linked view of database* of the "Thrive Tasks" database. Choose a table view. Hide the database title and name this view "Late Tasks ". Display the following properties.

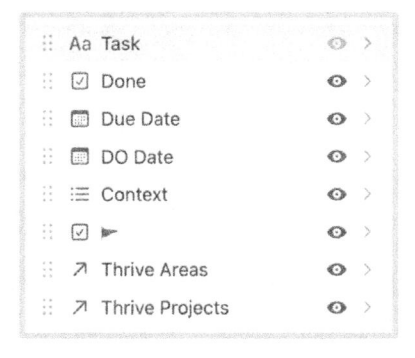

![Properties list: Task, Done, Due Date, DO Date, Context, (checkbox with flag), Thrive Areas, Thrive Projects]

Filter by Late = "checked" and "Done" is "unchecked" Sort descending by "Due Date". The view should look something like the below image.

![Task | Reports, Late Tasks view showing columns Task, Done, Due Date, DO Date, Context, with row "Thrive task 1", October 18, 2023, February 5, 2024]

105

6: Dashboards

7.2) Duplicate the previous view, call this one "Overdue (DO)". Removed the Late filter. Filter by "DO Date" is before today. Sort by "DO Date", descending.

7.3) Duplicate the previous view, call this one "Flagged". Remove the DO Date filter. Filter by "Flagged" is "checked".

7.4) Duplicate the previous view, call this one "All Tasks". Leave only the filter "Done" is "unchecked. Sort by "Task Age", descending.

7.5) Duplicate the previous view, call this one "Task Inbox". Leave the filter "Done" is "unchecked. Add the filter "Thrive Project" is empty and "Thrive Area" is empty. Sort by "Task Age", descending.

The view should look like the image below.

Tasks

Task | Reports

| Late Tasks | Overdue (DO) | Flagged | All Tasks | Task Inbox |

Aa Task	Done	Due Date	DO Date	Context	
Thrive task 1	☐	October 18, 2023	February 5, 2024		☐

8) Next, we will add our Task Insights, this will be the same view have in our Today Dashboard.

8.1) In Thrive Dashboard under the *Task Insights header*. Insert a *linked view of database* for "Thrive Insights". Choose the Gallery view, with large tiles. Hide the database name and filter "Name" = "Task". Make the following properties visible.

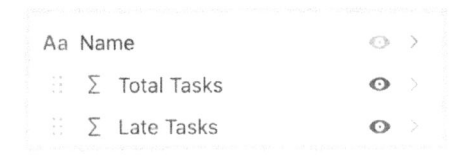

Aa Name	👁 >
∑ Total Tasks	👁 >
∑ Late Tasks	👁 >

The view itself should look like the below image.

The view itself should look like the below image.

```
Task | Insights
🎞 Gallery

Task Insights
Total tasks: 3
Late tasks:1
```

9) The next space is for ad-hoc reports. We will add the number of tasks per project.

9.1) In Thrive Dashboard under the *Tasks per Project header*. Add a linked view of the database for "Thrive Projects". Choose table view and hide the database name.

9.2) Add the display of the properties "Name", "Status" and "# Tasks". Order by "# Tasks", descending and filter on just active or on-hold projects. The view should look like the below image.

```
Tasks per Project
⊞ Tasks per Project

↓ # Tasks ∨    Status: In progress, On h... ∨   + Add filter

   Project Name          Status           # Tasks
   Thrive Project        ● ACTIVE         2
+ New
```

That is our GTD dashboard complete. Well, done.

Don't forget to link back to this dashboard from your "Today dashboard".

Summary

You now have dashboards that display your Thrive systems data more clearly. More importantly you can now see what you need to do, when you need to do it or review it. I hope this final chapter helped bring it all together. If you're feeling confident, why don't you try these final challenges.

Challenge 6: Create a weekly planner dashboard that uses a Calendar view of Thrive tasks for the next 7 days. You can do this in its own page for a weekly plan or add it to your Today page.

Challenge 7: Create an area for your notes/references into your dashboards to complete your full view of a PARA system.

Summary

Bringing it all together, I hope you enjoyed learning and doing.

"Summarize, then act. The essence of productivity is knowing what to pursue next."

Anonymous

And that is as they say it, is that. You've now explored all the key areas and gained practical tools to use right away. From the basics of using Notion in Part 1, to creating custom apps with databases in Part 2, and finally, building a comprehensive personal task management system in Part 3. Remember to build upon and refine these concepts, and don't skip the challenges—they're designed to help solidify your learning.

The main goal was to inspire you and provide a foundation of ideas and tools that you can adapt to your unique needs. No longer must you conform to the limitations of a standard to-do app. With Notion, you can create exactly what you need to excel. So, go ahead—experiment, enjoy, and achieve great things.

References

Top tips

Create new page:

Mac: **Cmd+Shift+Enter**

Windows: **Ctrl+Shift+Enter**

Move blocks around:

For a Mac: **Cmd + shift + click**

Windows: **Shift + click**

Toggle Sidebar:

Mac: **Cmd + **

Windows: **Ctrl + **

Search:

Mac: **Cmd + P**

Windows: **Ctrl + P**

Add Comment:

Mac: **Cmd + Shift + M**

Windows: **Ctrl + Shift + M**

Block types:

Chapter 2 explained block types, here's more detailed information:

Text blocks (also described in Chapter 2): The most basic Notion block is the Text block, which is used for simple text input. You can use Text blocks for headings, paragraphs, and lists. Notion also supports Markdown syntax, so you can format your text using headings, bold, italics, and other styles.

Media blocks: Notion also supports a variety of media blocks that allow you to embed images, videos, audio files, and other types of media directly into your notes. You can also use these blocks to embed content from external sources like YouTube, Vimeo, and SoundCloud.

Database blocks: One of the most powerful features of Notion is its support for databases. With a Database block, you can create tables of data and customize the fields to match your specific needs. This is particularly useful for managing tasks, projects, and other types of structured data. We will cover these in more detail in the next chapter.

Embed blocks: Notion also supports Embed blocks, which allow you to embed content from external websites and services directly into your notes. You can use Embed blocks to embed anything from a Google Calendar to a Trello board to a Twitter feed.

Divider blocks: Used to separate sections of content within a page. You can use them to visually break up your notes and make them easier to read and navigate.

Database data types:

Text: The text data type allows you to enter any kind of alphanumeric characters. It is the most basic data type and can be used for things like names, descriptions, or any other textual information.

Number: The number data type is used for storing numerical values. You can use it for things like quantities, prices, ratings, or any other numeric data.

Select: The select data type allows you to create a predefined list of options and choose one from them. For example, you can create a select property for "Status" with options like "To Do," "In Progress," or "Done." This data type is useful for categorizing and filtering your data.

Multi-Select: The multi-select data type is like select, but it allows you to choose multiple options from a predefined list. For example, you can have a multi-select property for "Tags" with options like "Work," "Personal," or "Urgent." This data type is helpful when you want to assign multiple categories or labels to an item.

Date: The date data type enables you to store specific dates or date ranges. Notion provides a calendar picker that allows you to choose dates easily. You can use this data type for deadlines, events, or any time-related information.

Checkbox: The checkbox data type represents a Boolean value (true or false). It is commonly used for creating to-do lists or marking items as completed. You can toggle the checkbox on or off to indicate the status of an item.

Relation: The relation data type establishes a connection between two databases or tables. You can use it to link related information across different databases. For example, if you have a database for projects and another for team members, you can create a relation property in the projects database to associate team members with each project.

File: The file data type allows you to attach files to your database entries. You can upload documents, images, or any other file type. This data type is useful when you want to store additional files or resources related to your data.

URL: The URL data type is used for storing website addresses or links. It automatically converts the text into clickable links, making it convenient for referencing external websites or resources.

Email: The email data type is designed to store email addresses. It validates the format of the email address and provides a clickable link to open the default email client with the address pre-filled.

Formula: The formula data type allows you to perform calculations or manipulate data based on the values of other properties in the same database. You can use formulas to automate calculations, generate summaries, or derive insights from your data.

These are the main data types available in Notion databases. By utilizing these data types effectively, you can create powerful and versatile databases to organize and analyze your information in various ways.

Overview of Synced Blocks

Synced blocks, which were not covered in this book, allow users to replicate the same content across multiple pages or areas within a workspace. This feature is particularly useful for maintaining consistent information across different documents without the need to update each block manually every time a change is made. I used this to write this book, with each chapter being in its own pages and then bringing them together as synchronized blocks across the whole book.

How to Create Synced Blocks

1. **Initiate a Synced Block:** To start, simply type `/sync` into a new block in Notion, which brings up the option to create a synced block.
2. **Input Content:** Once you create a synced block, you can add any content such as text, images, or to-do lists. This content will be the master copy that you can replicate elsewhere.

Expanding Synced Blocks

- **Duplicate Elsewhere**: To duplicate the synced block on another page, copy the block as you would with any other content in Notion. Then, navigate to the new location and paste it. The block will retain a link to the original, and any changes made will reflect across all instances.
- **Identifying Synced Blocks:** Synced blocks are easy to identify as they have a distinct border and a sync icon, signaling that they are linked to another source.

Practical Uses of Synced Blocks

- **Team Collaboration:** Synced blocks are incredibly useful for teams, ensuring that everyone has the latest updates without requiring multiple communications or manual updates.
- **Template Information:** For templates that are used repeatedly, such as meeting agendas or project trackers, synced blocks can ensure that every instance of the template starts with the same base information.
- **Resource Management:** Manage resources like guidelines, codes of conduct, or branding materials that need to be consistent across various company documents.

Tips for Using Synced Blocks

- **Review Regularly:** While synced blocks reduce the need for frequent updates, it's important to review them periodically to ensure the information is still relevant and accurate.
- **Use Sparingly:** Overusing synced blocks can make your workspace difficult to navigate. Use them strategically for information that truly needs to be consistent across multiple areas.

Limitations

- **Editing Restrictions:** When editing a synced block, be mindful that changes affect every instance of that block. This is beneficial for consistency but can be problematic if changes are made inadvertently.

Advanced Tips

- **Nested Syncing:** You can nest synced blocks within other synced blocks for complex documents but be cautious as this can get confusing if not managed properly.
- **Linking External Data:** While Notion doesn't directly support live external data syncing within blocks, you can use integrations or embeds to show updated data from external sources.

Synced blocks in Notion streamline the management of repeated content across multiple pages, making them an essential feature for users looking to maintain consistency in collaborative environments or across numerous documents.

Books mentioned in this book

- Getting Things Done: The Art of Stress-Free Productivity, David Allen, Penguin books.
- Building a Second Brain, Tiago Forte, Penguin books – covers the PARA system.
- Eat That Frog, Brain Tracy, Berrett-Koehler.
- The Pomodoro Technique, Francesco Cirillo.
- 1-3-5 method is not covered in a book, but one good article can be found here: https://www.timedoctor.com/blog/1-3-5-rule/

Other book recommendations

- Deep Work: Rules for Focus Success in a Distracted World, Cal Newport, Grand Central Publishing
- The 7 Habits of Highly Effective People: Powerful Lessons in Personal Change, Stephen Covey, Free Press.

About the author

Bronek is a highly experienced management consultant, non-executive director, technologist, and self-declared productivity geek. With over 20 years of experience delivering large-scale project changes, across multiple industries for IBM and now a global boutique consultancy.

His passion for productivity is driven by the challenges of juggling professional commitments, personal projects, and family life. Delivering more himself and for his clients. Bronek is also a dedicated coach and mentor, having facilitated numerous training sessions primarily focused on project management. His approach is rooted in practicality, aiming to empower professionals and himself to achieve their highest potential.

Contact Bronek at bronek@infinitypublishing,co.uk